THE JEWISH MORNING JOURNAL
THE ONLY JEWISH MORNING PAPER

דער מאָרגען זשורנאל

הײַנט

מאָמענט

פֿאלקסצײט

MORNING FREIHEIT
פֿרײַהײט

Forward
פֿאָרװערטס

THE PRIME OF YIDDISH

by

DAVID PASSOW

Copyright © Gefen Publishing House
Jerusalem 1996/5756

All rights reserved. No part of this publication may be translated, reproduced, stored in a retrieval system or transmitted, in any form or by any means, electronic, mechanical, photocopying, recording or otherwise, without express written permission from the publishers.

Typesetting: Marzel A.S. – Jerusalem

Cover Design: Gil Friedman / Gefen

Edition 9 8 7 6 5 4 3 2 1

Gefen Publishing House Ltd. Gefen Books
POB 6056, Jerusalem 12 New St., Hewlett
91060 Israel N.Y., U.S.A. 11557

Printed in Israel

Send for our free catalogue

Library of Congress Cataloging-in-Publication Data

Passow, David, 1918-

The prime of Yiddish: the language of Jewish ideas and ideologies / David Passow

p.   cm.

ISBN 9652291528

1. Niger, Samuel, 1883-1955. 2. Yiddish language. 3. Jews—Languages. 4. Jews—Intellectual life 5. Judaism—20th century. 6. Authors, Yiddish—Biography. I Title.

PJ5111.5.N54P37 1996   437'.947—dc20   96-1786
                                                          CIP

Contents

Preface 5

Introduction 6

Chapter I   Yiddish in the Goldene Medine 9

Chapter II   The Yiddish Press in America 19

Chapter III   Samuel Niger – an intellectual profile 33

Chapter IV   Yiddish vs. Hebrew – Kulturkampt 39

Chapter V   Bi-Lingualism in Jewish literature 49

Chapter VI   Yiddish enters the mainstream 57

Chapter VII   The Czernowitz Conference 65

Chapter VIII   Two new Jewish population centers 79

Chapter IX   Jewish Secularism 87

Epilogue 114

Afterword 119

Index of Names 121

Index of Publications 123

Acknowledgement

Sincerest thanks to the YIVO Institute for Jewish Research, New York City, for making available much of the background material in this study.

*For Aviva, Judah, Mimi, Shammai –
who made life worthwhile.*

Preface

It is unlikely that in the year 1900 even the most keen-sighted and prescient observer could have foreseen that before the new century had run half its course, Jewish life in the central and eastern parts of Europe, where the largest and most creative Jewry in the world had been concentrated for ages, would be almost completely annihilated. Nor could he have predicted that some six million Jews – a third of the total world Jewish population – would be swept away in a cataclysmic tragedy whose magnitude and horror beggar description, and before which all previous misfortunes in the millennial history of Jewish suffering pale into relative insignificance. Historical hindsight might lend the catastrophe a semblance of inevitability, but the supposition that it could have been anticipated in anything approximating its actual form, or that it might have been prepared for, seems altogether gratuitous.

Yiddish, no more the language of that vital, intelligent and driven society, still hovers over yesterday's horizon and evokes a stream of consciousness that combines nostalgia, introspection, imagination and cultural reminiscences. The issue, however, must not be seen as one of continuity or identity. Most memorable cultural achievements were created in tongues of periods different from the present: the languages of Greek tragedy or Hebrew poetry in medieval Spain are no longer alive today; the world of Shakespeare is certainly not our contemporary milieu. Closed chapters of history, they offer masterpieces of culture, relevant to us as fictional universes that enlarge our spectrum of imagination and sense of the past. Yiddish culture was a peak of Jewish creativity in the last two thousand years. It may have no continuity in the future, but it is interesting and rewarding for its own sake.

This study will deal with an incredibly brief segment of time – from the middle of the 19th century to post World War II – that streaked across the heavens of Jewish history like a meteor. The extraordinary pace and extent which characterized the development and sophistication of Yiddish cultural productivity in this capsulized period has no parallel in the saga of modern man.

It will also concentrate on one of the most creative and innovative personalities of the period, whose scholarship, intuition, and intellectual integrity contributed so extensively to the enhancement of Yiddish culture – in short, "the times of Samuel Niger."

As if by some grand design, the flight of East European Jews to the New World created vibrant centers of cultural and intellectual growth even while the European Jewish population was being decimated by pogroms, revolutions and war. Withal that, the urge to create was never stilled and somehow managed to incise itself ineradicably into the cultural annals of the Jewish people.

Jerusalem
May 5, 1995
ה' אייר תשנ"ה

Introduction

Samuel Charney was born in Dukor (near Minsk, Russia) on the 17th day of Tammuz (July 21) 1883. He had the traditional Hebrew education of that time, having studied first in the *yeshiva* (school for rabbinic studies) in Berezin and then in Minsk, where he came in contact with the Zionist and Socialist movements. Just before he was to receive *s'michah* (ordination) in 1900, he abandoned rabbinic studies and turned to illegal propaganda work on behalf of the *Poale Zion* (Labor Zionist) group with which he had become affiliated. At that point he assumed the surname Niger.

After arrest and imprisonment he participated in the founding of the *Zionist Socialist Party* in Odessa and became its leader in 1904. His literary career was launched in earnest with contributions to various party organs. He also turned his attention to one of his prime interests – belles lettres.

Following the abortive Russian revolution of 1905, Niger, like so many of his contemporaries, turned from political to literary activity. The journal, *Literarishe Monetshrift* (Literary Monthly) which he founded in 1908, together with *A. Veiter* (Eisic Meir Devenishki [1878-1919]), and *Shmarye Gorelik* (1877-1942), epitomized the renaissance of Yiddish literature and stamped him as a champion of the movement for the elevation of Yiddish as a literary instrument.

Nevertheless, at the historic *Czernowitz Language Conference* in 1908, which centered around the debate whether Yiddish was to be proclaimed as *the* or *a* national language of the Jewish people, Niger adopted a middle course between the Yiddishists and Hebraists. He did not denigrate the significance of Hebrew literature but claimed for Yiddish the right to give literary expression to the awakening Jewish consciousness. In effect, he became a leader of the Yiddishists and his journal the organ of Yiddish literary renascence. He paid homage to the classics while concentrating on encouraging young writers. Concurrently he gained ever broader recognition as a serious critic.

1917 was a turning point in Niger's life because it heralded the fulfillment of both his dreams of democracy – in Russia by means of the February revolution and in Zionism through the Balfour Declaration. Thus his articles in *Kultur un Bildung* (Culture and Education) and later in *Di Voch* (The Week) reflected the impact of the democratic February revolution that seemingly introduced an era conducive to autonomism and highlighted the conflict between the radical internationalism of Communism and the various schools of Jewish nationalism.

Consequently the question of bi-lingualism assumed increasing importance in Niger's writings, as did matters of Zionism and Marxism vis-à-vis the approach to Jewish problems. In 1918 Niger went from Petrograd to Moscow and then on to Vilna, Lithuania, where, for a while, he edited the daily *Der Tog* (The Day).

He emigrated to the United States in October 1921. After a brief association with the Socialist *Forward* he joined the staff of *Der Tog* (New York) and began a series of columns and literary critiques which continued to the end of his life in 1955.

Because of his erudition, sensitivity, profundity, literary ability and productivity, Niger was recognized as pre-eminent among commentators on secularist Jewish thought and Yiddish letters. The thriving Yiddish press in the United States to which he was a consistent contributor and whereby he reached tens of thousands of readers almost daily, enabled him to affect the intellectual climate that obtained among large segments of the Jewish public. As a literary critic for the cognoscenti he inspired an entire generation of Yiddish writers and set new and higher standards for them. Niger's literary creativity must be viewed in light of his credo: traditionalism with secularist overtones, bi-lingualism and the uniqueness of the Jewish people. He saw no contradictions inherent in these concepts nor did he set an order of precedence. Throughout his career these components were treated and categorized in varying sequence depending upon the urgency of the moment. However, at no time did he abandon his conviction that the singular Jewish contributions to civilization are a deep source of pride to the Eternal People.

Toward the end of his days Niger understood that no one could anticipate a rosy future for Yiddish, because it was no longer a vital culture. Gone were schools which employed it as the language of instruction, as well as the vibrant communities whose vernacular it was. In the past, worldly Jews would abandon their religious atmosphere and gravitate towards secular, Yiddishist circles. Currently, he maintained, and particularly since the establishment of the State of Israel in 1948, the overarching preference was for Hebrew. True, there was a superficial interest in Yiddish as manifested by specific faculties functioning on the several university campuses, but none of them carried on intrinsic research in what once was Yiddish culture.

This study will attempt to paint a portrait of a man whose creative career spanned this brief, kaleidoscopic period in Jewish cultural history against a background of the intellectual and cultural trends which obtained. He epitomized those unique talents which flowered – and withered – with the emergence, efflorescence, and destruction of one of the most glorious moments in Jewish annals.

Chapter I

In 1881 some eight million Jews lived in Europe, about five million in Czarist Russia, two million in the Austro-Hungarian empire, half a million in Germany, quarter of a million in Rumania, and the rest mainly in Western Europe. The Jews of Russia, Austria and Eastern Prussia were mostly descendent from their forebears who had lived in Poland before the several partitions at the end of the eighteenth century. In all three empires, which were ruled by enlightened despots with absolute power, the Jews were subjected to discriminatory decrees and persecution.

In 1815, when Poland was annexed by Russia, the Jews were herded into a Pale of Settlement and forbidden to move into the interior of their new country. They were expelled from villages, prevented from living in big cities, disproportionately taxed and excluded from occupations in which they had been engaged for centuries. They suffered a variety of harassments and discriminatory policies intended to bring about their conversion or to erase their Jewish distinctiveness: compulsory long-term military service, restrictions on accepted Jewish attire, obligatory attendance at secular schools, excessive taxes on kosher meat and ritual candles, prohibitions on Yiddish and Hebrew publishing, and widespread censorship.

The Jews in Russia and Congress Poland, that part of central Poland that had been formed out of the Duchy of Warsaw, shared in the ferment of the period, its political upheavals, economic vicissitudes, and cultural changes. Perhaps the most striking factor of Jewish existence at the time was biological. Jewish fertility in the eighteenth and nineteenth centuries increased dramatically. The Jewish population grew tenfold under Russian rule, exceeding that of the non-Jewish rate. This extraordinary Jewish increase was undoubtedly due to the unprecedentedly low mortality among Jews, both infant and adult. The combination carried well into the twentieth century, with the result that the Jewish population in Eastern Europe continued to burgeon, despite unrelenting depletions by emigration.

That enormous population growth, especially in the Pale of Settlement and the hinterlands of Galicia, where industrial backwardness and primitive agriculture produced economic stagnation, sapped the financial resources of the Jews and narrowed their productive opportunities. Conventional Jewish occupations were in trade and handicrafts. They were modest entrepreneurs, artisans and journeymen in the clothing crafts (tailoring, cap-, shoe-, bootmaking, hosiery, furriery), in textile weaving, carpentry and masonry. They were goldsmiths, silversmiths, blacksmiths, bakers, butchers, vintners, carters, drivers, day laborers, innkeepers and estate managers. Eastern Europe's retail and wholesale trade, from the big grain and timber merchants down to the itinerant peddlers, were largely in Jewish hands. They were agents, factors, brokers for agricultural produce and manufactured goods. As intermediaries between country and city, they brought the peasants' produce to the cities and returned to the rural areas with manufactured goods.

It should be noted that the Jews maintained a largely autonomous social and cultural existence. Their religious, educational and charitable institutions were structured and directed by the *kehillah* (Hebrew: community, congregation), an oligarchy of wealthy, learned and self-appointed leaders. However, under the pressure of absolutist and despotic rulers, it was assigned tasks that were not intended to serve the needs of the Jewish community but rather the exigent demands of the oppressive regime. Thus the impoverished Jew regarded it as the instrument of a hostile government, thereby bringing about the gradual decline of conventional authority in the community.

Early in the nineteenth century, Hasidism swept through Jewish Eastern Europe, capturing the loyalties of most Jews while leaving embattled and embittered supporters of normative rabbinic Judaism in beleaguered urban enclaves, especially Vilna and elsewhere in Lithuania. Hasidism constituted a social as well as religious revolution by overturning the authority of rabbis learned in Jewish precepts as it elevated the charismatic rebbes (Hasidic leaders) and their oral teachings.

In effect, Hasidism in its own way began to change the sanctioned structure of rabbinic authority in the Jewish community. It also brought to the little man greater awareness of his own self-worth.

However, the greatest assault against tradition came from the Western influences that penetrated into Eastern Europe – from Vienna into Galicia, and from Prussia into Lithuania and Latvia. This almost irresistible force of secularist enlightenment brought secular learning into a world that had been shaped and guided by Talmudic learning.

In the second half of the nineteenth century this new direction appeared among Jews in the guise of revolutionary, populist movements. Young Jews, university trained and professionally qualified, especially those who were deeply bruised by the pariah status of Jews in Russian society, were attracted by this heady idea, for it promised to destroy the hated social order and replace it with a new society, predicated on equality and fraternity. Toward the end of the century, this trend gave rise to several Jewish offshoots that were not only animated by the drive to reorder Russia's social and political structure, but were specifically aimed at solving the anomaly of Jewish existence; to make them equal participants in the host society, yet free to develop their own cultural and national existence.

Anti-Semitism had been a constant in Eastern Europe. Since the Polish partitions, restrictive, discriminatory regulations and laws were the familiar expression of that animosity. A new phenomenon, the pogrom, manifested itself first during Easter 1871 in Odessa, the newest, most cosmopolitan and liberal city in the empire with minimal anti-Semitism, a place where Jews were assimilated, Russified, and more at ease than anywhere else. That pogrom was a harbinger of things to come by demonstrating that the inhospitality of the Czarist regime, and indeed of all Russian society to the presence of Jews among them, was based not on Jewish poverty or separatism. It simply proved that even those Jews who met the criteria of the Russifiers were just as vulnerable to persecution as were their poor and unacculturated brethren.

Consequently, Jews began to flee from their homes and country, desperate to escape the raging violence and horror unleashed against them by their rulers. That precipitous and unpremeditated flight turned into a mass exodus, for even as the authorities stopped fomenting pogroms against Jews, they embarked on a more systematic form of persecution that could be described as an "administrative pogrom." In May 1882 the infamous May Laws were enacted, designed not only to deprive Jews of their livelihoods in Russia, but to make their continued presence intolerable. Almost every aspect of their lives was affected: places of residence, economic and educational opportunities, civic status. These regulations demonstrated with calculated contempt and cruelty that Jews would have no future in Russia. Thenceforth, until the outbreak of World War I in 1914, except for the brief interlude of the abortive 1905 Revolution, Jewish life in Russia was marked by cycles of violent pogroms and governmental persecution. What had begun as a stream of Jewish refugees in flight from terror in 1881 turned into a flood tide of mass migration.

A pogrom is a catastrophe or earthquake. It is not of long duration. The beast in man subsides quickly and crawls back into its cave. It was, therefore, highly essential that Jews be thoroughly familiar with their enemies. Through introspection they could have had intensity, durability and courage, enabling them to resist the vagaries of life. By understanding the strengths and weaknesses of their foes they would have been better equipped to do battle, thus assuring the survival of the Jewish people. Yet realistically, hunger, pogroms, and the fear of death were like blunt needles stuck into their souls, a condition many could no longer recall; a memory suppressed in their consciousness.

The capacity for forgetting is extremely valuable and often a balm for the spirit. Between pogroms in the Ukraine and Poland, Jews erected children's homes, institutions, libraries, synagogues, hospitals for the chronically ill and schools. Weddings took place. Had they not forgotten that which had occurred, their surge for self-preservation would have shrivelled and they would have perished as a people.

Yet one must carefully weigh the serious reservations concerning the equanimity of pogrom victims. Did they really efface the past from their consciousness or did they merely sublimate it with a frenetic lunge toward relocation and rehabilitation? Perhaps it might have been psychologically sounder to articulate the fear and depression they harbored rather than to appear poised and normal on the earth which so recently reverberated with the agonizing cries of their brethren.

Thus, in the mind of European Jews, the escape hatch, America, had long been universally perceived as a symbol of freedom, a beacon of liberty and equality. Indeed, it represented the same to millions of immigrants who had come from all over Europe since the seventeenth century. It was the "New World," fresh with possibilities that no longer existed in the old. It was the "golden land," rich in opportunity to work, eat, and make a more comfortable life for oneself than in the bleakness of the abandoned home. America beckoned with the future, while Europe was mired in the past.

America offered a vision of a land without prejudices, freed from the chains of tradition. It was without the encumbrances of bygones, the fixities of established society, the distinctions of caste and class. One of Sholem Aleichem's characters extolled America as "the only land of real freedom and real equality. In America you can sit right here and next to you will sit the President." America, he said, was the land of opportunity: "All the millionaires and billionaires in America worked hard and long when they were young. Some in the shop and some on the street. Ask Rockefeller, Carnegie, Morgan, Vanderbilt, what they once were. Didn't they sweep the streets? Didn't they sell newspapers? Didn't they shine shoes for a nickel?"

To be sure, voices were raised that spoke of America not as the "*goldene medine*" (the golden land), but as the "*treyfene medine*" (the impure land), the place where Judaism could not and did not thrive, where the Sabbath was violated, where *kashrus* (dietary laws) and *Yidishkayt* (Jewishness) could not withstand the winds of freedom. There were even some, but not very many, who spurned America for a return to Zion. A proto-Zionist movement began to take shape in those days among young, Russified Jews whose Jewish identity had been stirred into awareness by the pogroms. A few hundred undertook the hazardous journey to Palestine to settle in the ancestral land and to reclaim the recalcitrant soil with the labor of their own hands.

But most Jews who wanted to leave Russia, Galicia and Rumania set their course for America. Those who came between 1881 and 1914 were in search of opportunity and freedom in the New World, eager for that new start and life that America symbolized.

The Jews who fled their homes and towns in the Russian Pale right after the pogroms of April 1881, the impoverished Jews from the backwater towns and villages of Galicia, and the persecuted Jews of Rumania who set off on foot toward America, were all cut from the same cloth. They were young; at first most of them were men, later also young women joined the exodus; still later young families began to emigrate. For the most part they were vigorous and adventurous, physically able to endure the long and difficult journey that they usually undertook with few, if any, funds. Sons and daughters left parents behind; they were eager to depart, ready to test their strength, to earn their independence, to enter new worlds and find broadening experiences. The impulse to emigrate was stimulated by a sense of despair and persecution, but, actually, a deeper source was the restless energy of young people discontented with their lot. This perception of thwarted aspirations was, of course, greatest among the poor and lowly. Those who owned property, had solid occupations or professions, who maintained themselves despite oppressive restrictions and regulations, were the least likely to emigrate. Why abandon one's home and position, ties and connections? Among the uneasy and distressed, the most avid emigrants were those who wished to break away from the watchful eyes of their elders and escape the prescribed patterns of behavior set by the traditional community; who were ready to abandon the 613 religious precepts because they resented the condescension of those Jews with status and their contempt of Jews without learning.

These emigrants had confidence in themselves – once they were rid of the age-old curse of anti-Semitism and had jettisoned the class distinctions of the traditional Jewish community. They hoped with boundless optimism that in the New World they would be on their way to success and prosperity, to that better life toward which all Jews strove. They were, characteristically, the new Americans.

In effect, this was a response to the immutable impact of enlightenment. Subtly, knowledge of the wider world had crept into the stifling villages. Secular books, bearers of new facts, ideas and visions had broken through the closed circle of the old study halls and left young men with new hopes. They sensed that there were alternatives to the endlessly repetitive life of poverty and persecution they led. Although options shone many miles distant, the road lay open and they had only to follow it. The stream steadily swelled as conditions that had produced it grew worse. In the climactic outburst of the nine years before World War I, one and a quarter million Jews, one seventh of all those in Europe, left it.

Great numbers took the same route as other displaced Europeans and landed in America. For those who made the total break, there were, from time to time, choices – Western Europe, England, South America, South Africa. Palestine attracted Zionists and, earlier, participants in the *Bilu* movement. But through the nineteenth and twentieth centuries the United States consistently was the destination of the largest number. For most Jews on the move, the land of opportunity was across the Atlantic. In that respect, they were like all other peoples in the surge of immigration away from Europe. The curve of Jewish flight to the United States runs remarkably parallel to that of the general immigration tide, an indication that the decisive, compelling forces were characteristic of the overall mass migration phenomenon.

It should be noted that in the latter years of the nineteenth century Jews had been a minority among emigrants from central Europe, far outnumbered by non-Jewish artisans and traders. But in Eastern Europe they were almost alone as such, and were first to make the move. In Galicia, for instance, where Jews were only twelve percent of the population, they represented sixty percent of the immigrants between 1881 and 1890. Peasants from that part of the continent later came in large numbers, but not until the turn of the century. The fact that these Jews arrived first among their co-nationals would significantly influence the course of their Americanization.

The numbers involved in this period of Jewish migration were also much greater than before 1870. In a single year, 1906, over 150,000 arrived in the United States, more than came in any decade before the Civil War. In the years between 1870 and 1914, the entries exceeded two million, of whom in excess of sixty percent originated in Russia, and over twenty percent in Austria-Hungary.

World War I caused an interruption which allowed less than a hundred thousand Jews to reach America in the course of the conflict. But the tide of Jewish emigration seemed about to resume when a quarter of a million crossed the Atlantic in the four years after 1920. Then, suddenly, the whole movement was choked off by a reversal of the liberal American attitude toward immigration in general.

A creeping sense of xenophobia, stimulated by nationalistic passions of the war years led, between 1920 and 1924, to the enactment of legislation which drastically curtailed the number of entries. A quota system based on nativity was imposed that excluded almost all South and East Europeans, among whom were the bulk of prospective Jewish migrants. In 1927 a new law further reduced the number for whom the gates remained open, and in 1930, an executive order effectively sealed all remaining chinks in the wall around the promised land. Although there were occasional relaxations in individual cases, as a rule the barriers were insurmountable. A whole era in American history had come to a close.

By then the American Jewish population was formed. The total had grown to almost four million in 1917 and to more than four and a quarter million in 1927. These were immigrants and their children whom war, persecution and, most of all, the fundamental economic dislocation of modern times, had summoned to a better life in a new world.

Like the Irish and other earlier immigrants in similar conditions, Jews turned to the rapidly expanding garment trades. Production shifted from the consumer's home, or shop of the custom seamstress and tailor, to the factory and machine. Men's coats and ladies' cloaks, shirts and blouses, hats and caps, fur mantles and silk ties, boned corsets and laced chemises, all were cheaply mass produced. The total value of the ready-made women's clothing industry output rose by 133 percent in the decade 1890-1900 alone. Jews became involved in the garment industries not by virtue of any proclivity for the needle or previous training, but because of the constant demand for cheap labor. Most of these were "Columbus tailors" (inexperienced), wedded to the "Katrinka" (a homely name for the sewing machine) once they reached the land of promise.

The precarious plight of the immigrant resulted, in a large measure, from the low wages characteristic of manufacturing that employed unskilled labor. The harsh reality was that before 1910 a man's work in the garment trades was not likely to yield more than twelve dollars a week when he worked. And what of the long periods of slack seasons and unemployment? It was an inescapable condition of the new life that the earnings of a single breadwinner could not support a household. Consequently, women and children were also compelled to enter the job market.

This circumstance made it somewhat easier for the Jewish immigrant to accept the ignominies of home work and the sweating system, by which laborers performed a single process at home on a piecework basis. Since, in any case, all family hands had to serve, it was better that they work together as a unit with their own kind, under circumstances that made it possible for them to observe the Sabbath, if so desired. In the dank, crowded tenements, dimly lighted whether by lamp or sun, the yards of cloth mounted up in heaps, waiting for tired fingers to transform them into the New World's fashions.

Toiling as they did in crammed quarters, at home or nearby, they clung to the illusion of independence. True, their working day was long and arduous, but perhaps with extreme exertion they could finally break through the darkness into the light of golden dreams. For some, behind the fantasy was a shred of reality – often just enough to keep hope alive. Hence, ultimately, the more fortunate were able to shuck their wage-earning status and become "businessmen." The popular image of the time ruled out pressers, for these, by common reputation, were uniformly a dull lot. But the ambitious cloakmaker could aspire to edge into the highly diversified organization of the industry as a contractor.

Although the largest portion of Jewish laborers were numbered in this particular field of manufacturing, there were many job seekers who sought employment in other pursuits. They found niches in a wide variety of manual operations, sometimes because of special skills they brought with them, but more often through the accident of acquaintanceship that revealed an opening or offered an entree into a trade. Some rolled cigars at home or in shops. Others labored in the building industry, for wages if they had to, or preferably for hire as independent glaziers, painters or carpenters. The more skilled found their living in the printing trades, fabrication of jewelry, the amusement business, and in an assortment of jobs as clerks and salespeople. Indeed, Jews were employed almost everywhere, except in heavy manufacturing, mining and agriculture.

Most Jews, like almost all other Americans in those years, faced the necessity of adjusting to a fundamental change. If native, they most likely were born and grew up in small towns of the rustic countryside. If immigrants, they came, in all probability, from tiny villages where even the ghetto bordered on open fields. Suddenly they were compressed into the narrow passages of great cities, stoned in from the sights of nature and crammed to overbursting with man-made objects. Only those who had experienced the pace of a European or American urban center were prepared for the newness of this life. Most had snatched passing glimpses of a thriving metropolis as they changed trains or moved through the seaports of London, Liverpool, Hamburg or Bremen, en route to the new world.

Inevitably, an ever increasing proportion of Jews in the United States were destined to live in major metropolitan regions. After 1890 about two-thirds of American Jewry would consistently reside in the four largest cities: New York (with about fifty percent), Chicago, Philadelphia and Boston. This concentration was due, somewhat, to their attractiveness for young men from the interior of the country, Jew and non-Jew alike; but in the final analysis, it was due to the massive immigration.

For the immigrant the area of primary settlement was often tolerable, but he soon perceived that he had others to consider. The effect of such a life was particularly harsh on those children born in America. Scornful of discipline in school, with parental authority weakened by the stigma of foreignness, driven into the streets because of overcrowding at home, they became anti-social. Too young they went off to work as newsboys or in shops, oblivious of the baleful influences upon them. The rate of juvenile delinquency was high, and even parents who did not read cold statistics knew their children were pagans, in danger of being lost.

Yet, despite the crushing poverty and dismal surroundings, the first generation of native American Jews produced a greater number of college graduates than any other ethnic group of immigrants who came during this period. Although relatively few attained this objective, the professions held a constant allure for Jews. The enormous expansion of such occupations seized their imagination. To the degree that doctors, dentists, lawyers, and teachers were usually trained in schools and not in apprenticeship, and more often appointed by examination than by favor, these professions became "free" – open to ability rather than family or personal contacts. Here, indeed, was a purpose worth slaving for. To immigrants the goal seemed close enough to be reached personally. By 1905 there were almost five hundred Jewish physicians in New York City alone. Many parents transferred their hopes to the next generation and toiled in the firm determination that they would open doors for their children. The vision of a son becoming a doctor or a lawyer kept many a man patiently at the treadle and blotted out the dismal environment in which he passed his days.

Chapter II

The history of Yiddish literature in America, which paralleled the rise of the Jewish labor movement and greatly affected its growth and influence, reflects, to a significant degree, the cultural development of Jewish workers. At the turn of the twentieth century a literature of broad scope was created, perhaps the most important non-English literature ever to arise in the United States. Simultaneous with the cultural progress of Jewish workers was a cultural evolution centering around the language. The *jargon*, as Yiddish was familiarly referred to, slowly became a literary instrument.

In its early phase, Yiddish literature in America was confined almost exclusively to journalism. About seventy Yiddish writers published their works in ephemeral journals of the last two decades of the previous century. Practically no writing of substance appeared in book form because authors generally sought publication in Europe, where printing was more accessible and cheaper. In the United States, the first Yiddish literary works were serialized in weeklies, and later, in dailies. Gradually, these periodicals began to free themselves from German and Germanized Yiddish which had dominated the early press. Nevertheless, a prominent publication, *Nu Yorker Yidishe Folkstzaytung* (New York Yiddish Folk-newspaper) promised to publish "interesting original stories and good translations of the most recent writers," as well as articles of general culture and movements in Jewish history, despite the fact that to keep that vow would prove to be as difficult as being both socialist and Jewish.

Thus the range of subjects treated in Yiddish expanded, giving more flexibility and richness to the language. There soon appeared popularizations of natural and social science subjects, as well as pieces on literary criticism and belles-lettres, thus widening readers' horizons and preparing them for material of a higher quality. Attracting intellectuals previously alienated from Yiddish was another important achievement for which the radical press was largely responsible. Writers and lecturers, whose language had been Russian, German or Hebrew, studied Yiddish in order to be read. Every important Jewish writer began his career by appearing in the Yiddish press, and eventually many became salaried employees of the different newspapers. Increasingly, the press originated and disseminated literature in all its forms. At first there was no distinction between journalism and belles-lettres, prose and poetry, and even one literary genre and another. All writing in the early radical press was essentially propaganda – literary artistry as such, was to come later.

During this period the popularization of higher Yiddish culture had often been criticized as being facile and superficial. However, long before a sophisticated, discerning audience could emerge, the mass of readers had to be educated in secular, contemporary matters and awakened to new interests. Samuel Niger summarized it pungently when he noted that "the Yiddish press in America was the midwife of Yiddish literature. If the Yiddish newspaper was a home (frequently, to be sure, an asylum) to the Yiddish writer, to the reader it was a *heder* (religious elementary class) if not a *yeshiva* (school for rabbinic learning). It taught him to read an unvocalized text, it gave him a taste for reading stories and poems in addition to the news, it enlightened him, it told him what was going on in the world, it gave him a certain degree of sophistication and an interest in social literature."

Within a few years of their landing in America, immigrants began to acquire strong cultural appetites. They searched out "literary evenings," poetry readings and story telling, which rapidly became a major folk institution. Soon newspapers brought the "literary evenings" into their homes by reprinting the works of European Yiddish writers and translations of non-Jewish classics. Due to the growing influence of Zionism, the didactic style and tone of writing was gradually loosened allowing for a greater interest in Jewish social and cultural problems, as well as that of national survival.

The term "Zionism" began to appear quite frequently at the turn of the century, but the movement as such was slow to affect Jewish life in the United States. Herzl's summons to the first Zionist Congress (1897) aroused less enthusiasm than criticism. Opposition soon surfaced as a conflict raged in the press and synagogue. The stand of Reform Judaism and the English dailies was most hostile. Zionism and its leaders were generally derided, satirized and discredited. Actually, American Zionism as a significant trend in Jewish life was not really apparent until World War I when Justice *Louis Brandeis* (1856-1941) gave the movement an American and humanitarian stamp. Even then, large segments of American Jewry remained anti-Zionist, or at best, non-Zionist. However, as the Yiddish press developed and attracted more talented writers, it became the sounding board for various opinions, thereby involving the Jewish community in what was ultimately to emerge as the most crucial issue of the time.

After the Kishinev pogroms in 1903, there was a substantial infusion of Zionist and Bundist literature from the pen of some outstanding commentators who challenged socialist shibboleths and emphasized the existence of the Jewish people. Thus, many began to think about their share of responsibility for continued Jewish development and the improvement of various cultural expressions. While for most Jewish radicals Jewish culture was merely a concept subordinate to cosmopolitan values and the class struggle, the succeeding waves of new immigrants – particularly the better educated and talented among them – demanded a heightened quality of Yiddish culture, particularly in literature and the theater. Hence the Yiddish dailies began to run a series of fictional sketches ranging from the simplest and most unpretentious to quite subtle and artistically rendered portrayals of life on New York's East Side.

Yet despite the attraction of these vignettes, no newspaper or journal could match the flesh-and-blood immediacy of the Yiddish theater. The socialist intellectuals knew that they could never displace it, although they found its repertory and influence cheap and trashy in the early days. Almost the whole ghetto poured into the three theaters on The Bowery – set in the midst of music halls, dives, shabby lodging houses, saloons and fake museums – the first four nights of the week, when blocks of seats were bought up by clubs, *Landsmanshaftn* (regional fraternal societies) and union locals. Crude melodrama, vaudeville tricks, and rubbishy historical spectacles were the usual fare. But the immigrant audience loved it. Many a poor Jew who made no more than ten dollars a week would spend five of it not only on the theater to see the play, which was his only source of amusement, but also to mingle with his friends and especially the actors, who strutted about in the cafes on Grand and Canal streets, fully aware of the adoring crowds whom they treated with haughty condescension or biting humor.

The heightened response to the Yiddish theater, human interest sketches, literary criticism and poetry, contributed enormously to the development of a literate audience and the beginnings of book acquisition. Although most books written before 1900 were novels of slight literary merit, mostly translations and adaptations, they broadened the immigrant reader's outlook and accustomed him to enjoy books as well as newspapers.

The interest in Yiddish cultural expression as a value in itself developed more fully in the early 1900s as Bundism, Zionism, and theories of Yiddish as a linguistic base for Jewish culture clashed with the older assumptions, and as a new wave of immigrants beat against the old. Yiddish resounded everywhere. The despised *jargon* was becoming a supple, rich, expressive instrument of permanent cultural value. It should be noted that whereas other ethnic groups became economically productive to the extent they were anglicized, Jews became so through Yiddish. In effect, Jewish productivity at the end of the nineteenth century meant proletarianization.

This economic transformation was made possible by the compactness of Jewish life within the ghettos of New York, Chicago, Philadelphia, and Baltimore. Jews worked for Jewish proprietors, as class conflicts took place in a Jewish atmosphere. Everyone spoke Yiddish. Frequently laborers and bosses came from the same town. Many shops were actually in the homes of employers, leading to occasional demands by workers for time off to attend religious services. A Jewish worker could live in a large metropolis for years and never come in contact with the non-Jewish world, nor have need for the English language. Jewish labor and capital may have battled on opposite sides of the economic barricades, but they lived within a common culture to a much greater degree than either would have been willing to admit.

Toward the end of the 19th century a number of writers arrived seeking a public platform for airing their ideologies. Nationalists, Socialists, orthodox Jews, Anarchists – all saw the Yiddish press as an important outlet for achieving their aspirations. Since most came from

Eastern Europe, they manifested hostility toward the central European Jew of Austro-German extraction and developed an intrinsically indigenous language compatible with the mentality and outlook of their land of origin.

Yiddish newspapers were assumed to be in a completely different category than non-Jewish publications. They were viewed as a living encyclopedia whose writers covered a broad spectrum of life, from leisure thinking to deep contemplation; casual conversation to a furrowed brow; advice for the entire household to a complex article concerning the secrets of creation; a joke, a poem, or a tale. Indeed, it was a combination of a home university and a house friend. In effect, the Yiddish press challenged the early waves of immigration and was largely responsible for organizing, orchestrating and perhaps even westernizing them. It started by teaching simple manners, polish and elegance, with a cosmopolitan or secularistic orientation. Most of all, it gave the immigrants a physiognomy all their own by making of them Socialists, Zionists, or Diaspora-Nationalists, while simultaneously urging them to strengthen their Jewish ties.

Most East European Jews came to the United States as political refugees, leading the Yiddish press to highlight the significance of proud citizenship in the new-found democracy. It became the exchange for ideas, thoughts, ideals, and political ideologies, like Socialism, with all its shadings, divisions, developments and new trends. It was a prime source of information and orientation in the Zionist world, as well as the organizing force within the Jewish community of all its fraternal, religious and social manifestations. It was through this medium that the working man became aware of his own interests thereby nudging him to establish trade unions and similar protective societies.

The halcyon days of the Yiddish press in America paralleled the period of the Russian revolution (1917-1920). The increased East European immigration in the first two decades of the 20th century was comprised primarily of younger people who had been subjected to a barrage of propaganda from various political parties in the old country. They were determined to rid themselves of the "cowering Jew" syndrome. Thus they became not only a levelling influence in the emerging trade union movement, but also added a modicum of modernization to communal work, and importance to the printed Yiddish word.

Nowhere in the world have so many Yiddish newspapers been sold as in the United States. This interesting statistic would suggest that the economic posture of the American Jewish immigrant was better than that of his brethren in Eastern Europe. Add to that the factor of concentrated urbanization. In 1930, there were 619,770 Yiddish speaking Jews in New York City – 50.7% of all foreign born who claimed Yiddish as their mother tongue. In Boston, Los Angeles, Newark, Philadelphia, Cleveland and Chicago there were 23.8%. Thus, 74.5% of the Yiddish speaking population living in eight cities, who were partial to an untrammeled press, represented the most likely purchasers of newspapers.

The first seventeen years of the century showed an approximately tenfold increase in circulation from about 66,000 in 1900 to about 646,000 in 1916. From 1917 to 1927 the number of sales levelled off and then began to decline steadily during the next thirteen years. The number of dailies also diminished during this timeframe. In 1916 there were eleven; 1927 to 1935 ten; 1936 to 1940 nine; by 1976 one – now there are none.

The situation was somewhat different with newspapers published in Philadelphia, Cleveland and Chicago. From 1904 until 1928 the number of buyers increased annually from 0.5% to 127.3%. In 1928 127 papers were sold for every ten in 1908. However, beginning with 1929, these publications suffered the same fate as all others in the country whose circulation declined at more or less the same rate.

Demand for newspapers was a direct function of the immigration rate to the United States. The number of newcomers declined from 272,268 in 1921-1924 to 67,686 in the period 1925-1930. From 1931-1939 105,580 arrived, or 38,000 less than in the single year of 1914. Concomitantly the percentage of Yiddish speakers diminished whereas the number of native Americans gradually increased. It is also likely that a significant number of immigrants had mastered English sufficiently to enable them to read an English publication.

The downward trend in circulation was also a byproduct of the economic depression. The sale of all American newspapers fell from 32.4 for every one hundred in the population in 1927 to 28 in 1933, while the Sunday editions dropped from 22.1 to 19.1. In 1933 the distribution of all American publications dropped to 13% less than in 1929. Yiddish newspapers lost more readers in 1932 and 1933 than in any other time during the depression period. This regression might also be attributed to the limited immigration.

The advent of radio should be considered a significant factor of circulation constriction, particularly as applied to the Yiddish press, inasmuch as Yiddish language programs became readily available in most metropolitan centers. In many instances the fare served as a surrogate for the newspapers.

The burgeoning circulation of the World War I years (1914-1918) led the prosperous newspapers already in existence to assert an ever increasing influence on their readership. It was at this point that *Der Tog* (The Day) began publishing in New York City; the *Yidishe Welt* (Jewish World) in Philadelphia; the *Yidishe Journal* (Jewish Journal) in Toronto and the *Yidishe Stimme* (Jewish Voice) in Los Angeles. The *Forward* inaugurated a special section in Chicago, including editions for the midwest and Pacific coast.

The *Forward*, whose daily circulation reached 206,000 (1919), was among the more successful newspapers since the turn of the 20th century. However, the most phenomenal progress, both materially and qualitatively, was achieved by *Der Tog*, in a large measure at the expense of *Die Wahrheit* (The Truth) which it had absorbed. The *Morgen Journal* (Morning Journal) developed significantly at the hand of *Jacob Saperstein*'s heir, *Israel Friedkin*, who took over after the *Tageblat* (Daily Bulletin), the outpost of orthodoxy, ceased publishing. In addition to replacing the *Tageblat* editorially, the *Morgen Journal* also acquired most of the classified advertising that had been the backbone of the now defunct paper. The *Yidishe Welt*, which started to publish in Philadelphia during the summer of 1914, represented the only Yiddish newspaper outside New York City (except for the *Chicago Courier*) that did not simply reprint news and editorial comments from "the majors." Yet despite the comparative success of the *Yidishe Welt*, the *Forward* still maintained a greater circulation in Philadelphia. It might be noted that the influence of the well established papers was in no way diminished by either the short-lived career of Poale Zion's *Di Zeit* (The Times), or the continued appearance of the Communist *Freiheit* (Freedom).

By the third decade of the century the Yiddish press logged most of its advertising from heavy industry and large commercial undertakings. The automotive manufacturers, who by this time produced a million cars annually, considered it sufficiently advantageous to run special sections in most of the major Yiddish newspapers. The front-runner in classified advertising was the *Morgen Journal* with an average daily income of approximately three thousand dollars.

Such a gratifying return made it possible to broaden extensively the news gathering and editorial components of the paper. Nevertheless, the amount of reading matter was determined by postal regulations which set a forty percent limit on advertising. The remaining percentage was taken as a challenge for enhancing the features quality in order to keep ahead in the circulation race.

By way of attracting and holding readership, the "big three" operated as follows: the *Forward* added a page or two to its daily edition. Thus the serious reader was compensated for the relatively larger portion of lighter material by the presence on staff of the leading belletristic writers of the time, among them *Sholem Asch* (1880-1957), *Yona Rosenfeld* (1880-1944), *I.J. Singer* (1893-1944), *H.D. Berkowitz* (1885-1967), *Zalman Schneour* (1887-1959), *Abraham Rosenfeld* (1846-1916), and *M. Osherowitz* (1888-1965). They were handsomely rewarded for the exclusive rights to segments of their writings before appearing in book form. At one point during this decade the editorial budget of the *Forward* reached $250,000 annually, while gross income was so great that by 1930 the *Forward* had accumulated a reserve fund of almost three million dollars.

Morris Weinberg, the first general manager of *Der Tog*, was largely responsible for its material success. His crowning ambition was to make it the most widely circulated Yiddish paper in the United States. Despite badgering the editorial department to broaden the popular material, he was, nevertheless, primarily responsible for adding to staff some of the most talented writers available, thereby justifying the logo on the masthead "*Der Tog* is the newspaper for the Jewish intelligentsia." Included in this group were *Samuel Niger* (1883-1955), *Dr. Abraham Coralnick* (1883-1937), *Dr. Chaim Zhitlovsky* (1865-1943), and *William Edlin* (1878-1947). In addition, Weinberg succeeded in bringing to America the leading journalist of Warsaw, *Samuel Rosenfeld* (1869-1943), who ultimately became a central figure in the editorial department of the paper.

Interestingly enough, *Der Tog* did not develop an impressive belletristic section. Aside from the few short stories and novellas by *Joseph*

Opatashu (1886-1954), and *Abraham Reisen* (1876-1953), *Leon Kobrin* (1872-1946) was their chief fiction writer for almost two decades. As a counter-balance, however, *Der Tog* included outstanding columnists, analysts and critics as an integral part of its editorial cadre. Thus the serious reader preferred this paper to the exclusion of most others.

Among the several significant, creative contributions to the Yiddish speaking world made by *Der Tog* was the complete *Yehoash* (*Yehoash Solomon Bloomgarden* 1872-1927) translation of the Bible. In addition, they also published the main portion of *Sholem Aleichem*'s (1859-1916) writings. During this decade, the annual editorial budget approximated $200,000.

In order to keep pace with the other two, the *Morgen Journal* consistently offered the largest amount of current news, gathered telegraphically. They also ran memoirs, diaries, biographies of outstanding Jewish personalities – mostly written by *Saul Safire* (1896-1965), who also contributed an extended, serialized novel. During this period the annual editorial outlay ranged between $100,000 and $150,000.

Thus readers of the Yiddish press were kept abreast of the American scene in particular, and the world in general, with, invariably, emphasis on the Jewish aspect. They were also barraged with a plethora of reading matter that included the best of contemporary Jewish literature as well as selections from the Jewish cultural past. The eclectic reader of more than one journal or newspaper would, therefore, be informed not only about recent events that interested him, but could also enjoy the elegance and scope of Yiddish.

Very few editors or writers shared *Abraham Cahan*'s (1860-1951) prescience about the Jewish fate in the offing. Despite his tenure as the veteran editor of a Socialist newspaper, he sensed, intuitively, the deep interest of the Jewish masses in the upbuilding of Palestine as a Jewish national home. He returned from a visit in 1926 fully "converted" to the importance of this aspiration to world Jewry. Ultimately he gave the *Forward* a pro-Zionist orientation and eliminated what Socialists called "Jewish paradoxicality." This about-face was all the more remarkable, inasmuch as the centrist papers had held that position from the turn of the century.

Starting with the 1890s the conflict between secularism and pietism, revolutionaryism and conservatism led the swelling ranks of radicals to conclude that the daily press was inadequate. Their attention turned to monthly journals which, in the main, were cooperatively owned. During this decade there appeared among others *Di Zukunft* (The Future), published by the Yiddish speaking section of the Socialist Workers Party of North America, edited by *Philip Krantz*. When it was absorbed by the *Forward Association* in 1913, *Abraham Liessen* (1872-1938) took over. In addition, there were *Di Freie Gezelshaft* (The Free Society), an avant-garde magazine issued by the Association of the same name, under the editorship of *M. Leontiev*; *Di Neie Zeit* (The New Time), put out by Yiddish speaking Socialists; *Der Neier Geist* (The New Spirit), an independent monthly for critique, literature and art, edited by *Alexander Harkavy* (1863-1939). Simultaneously the activist radicals attempted to publish a series of weeklies both in New York and the provinces. Included in the several projects undertaken were the *Socialistishe Arbeter Zeitung* (Socialist Workers Newspaper) and the anarchist *Freie Arbeter Shtimme* (Free Workers Voice), which, despite many vicissitudes, managed to appear well into the 1970s.

Obviously, the dailies had a considerably greater impact on the Jewish population. However, one should not minimize the importance of the weeklies and monthlies despite the fact that most were short-lived. Together with the dailies, and as an adjunct to forums, lectures, discussions, and symposia, these journals played an important role in enlightening the Jewish proletariat and raising their cultural level by disseminating information. The material dealt with was often opinionated, superficial, and the manner of presentation condescending. However, in view of the average immigrant's generally low plane of cultural receptivity, particularly with regard to worldly matters, any step towards arousing social or intellectual interest, expanding access to information concerning the natural and social sciences, constituted progress, even if the data were primarily educational or represented a call for solidarity in the struggle for better living conditions, social justice and freedom.

A significant achievement of the Yiddish press was that it managed to attract a group of intellectuals who previously had been alienated from Jewish life and its languge. Writers and lecturers who favored Russian, Hebrew, or German went over to Yiddish. Prior to this time there was an intelligentsia without a people and a people without an intelligentsia. By virtue of the Yiddish press and the socially oriented organizations and readers it represented, the intelligentsia without a people became a folk intelligentsia, and the population without an intelligentsia became an intellectually responsive readership. Thus dozens of creative people found a platform and an audience, while the culturally hungry masses discovered a means of gratification.

Starting with the 1880s Yiddish writers made a concerted effort to enhance the peculiarly Germanic quality of the language. As a consequence of the contemporary issues and ideas with which they dealt, there developed more sophisticated and colorful aspects of the language, resulting in a perceptible lexicographical enrichment plus stylistic modernization. Yiddish gradually became not only the language of and for mundane usage, but also a medium of expression for broader, deeper questions as well as a multifaceted and exact instrumentality which enabled writers to deal even with esoteric problems.

As it continued to evolve, the Yiddish press turned into the prime disseminator of Yiddish literature in a variety of forms. It was at once the pedagogue of both author and reader, teaching the former to write and the latter to read. Unlike non-Yiddish cultures, the Yiddish press was not a branch of literature but rather the source whence it sprang, by reprinting the classics as well as works of contemporary authors, most of whom had made their debut in America. Thus the reader was the beneficiary of the poets', critics', and short story writers' labors by virtue of the fact that almost every Yiddish tale, novel, poem or critical essay appeared originally in the press and only afterwards in book form.

At the turn of the twentieth century Yiddish literature was in essence journalism. The distinction was primarily in form and not content, inasmuch as no perceptible parameters had as yet been defined. There was a retreat to the previous age of syncretism thus eliminating lines of demarcation between the respective genres. This phenomenon applied as much to polemical articles as to scientific popularizations, short stories and poetry. The purpose was clearly enlightenment and education. Regardless of the format employed, whether journalistic or belletristic, prose or poetry, the point of departure was not the writer's position as much as the intellectual and moral stance of the readers. The objective was to offer new sources of information and the promulgation of ideas for confrontation rather than to provide an outlet for self-expression.

Thus in striving to turn the reading public's attention to specific trends or concepts, form became a medium. In some cases it transcended the importance of the content. In other instances it inadvertently had an aesthetic, artistic, and intellectual impact. This applied primarily to the poetry of the day which became an integral part of the working masses' song repertory.

Also characteristic of the time was the Yiddish press's propensity for combining informative with agitative journalism in both prose and verse. Perhaps this was a subconscious confluence with American literature which had turned basic journalistic reportage into an art form. The burgeoning circulation during the second decade of the twentieth century was not only a direct function of the massive immigration wave but also of a broadened cultural horizon; the proliferation of the trade union movement; the efflorescence of literature; the emergence of Zionism, and the growth of *Landsmanshaften* (townsfolk organizations).

The centrality of the Yiddish press in the social and organizational life of the Jewish masses loomed exceedingly large. Because of intensified competition between the different newspapers they invariably pandered to the lowest common denominator of the readership's taste in pursuit of economic advantages accruing from increased circulation. Nevertheless, publishers were influenced by the growing number of intelligent readers and competently qualified writers so that they printed more polemical articles, short stories and poems of a higher order. The press also played a signal role in the Americanization of the Jewish immigrant by encouraging him to show an interest in the political and economic life of his new home as well as providing him with opportunities for contact with other spheres of society. Likewise, by virtue of the torrent of news from the other side of the ocean, the press served as a constant reminder of the "old home" and its culture, thus arousing an intense feeling of nostalgia and a sense of responsibility so that one willingly extended a helping hand in time of need.

It is important to note that in its dedication to the Americanization process the impact of the Yiddish press was essentially in the direction of creating a configuration of Jewish life on American soil. Concurrently, there was substantial thrust towards building Jewish institutions and creating a distinctive life style. The *Landsmanshaften*, which emerged as a result of immigrant gregariousness, found in the press a deep source of solace. It was likewise a major factor in institutional and organizational fundraising. Jewish secular movements, particularly Zionism, Socialism, and Anarchism, found spokesmen who consistently addressed their respective constituencies. The press also played a vital role in the emerging Jewish trade union movement because of its persistent clamor for organization and the creation of a compatible atmosphere within the several strata of the Jewish body politic.

During the 1920s and into the 1930s, the Yiddish press acted as a gadfly and aroused public opinion to the point where the Jewish establishment was compelled to undertake aggressive courses of action on behalf of the community. The original protest march against pogroms in pre-World War I Poland was organized by the *Y.L. Peretz Writers Association*. The press was also the prime motivating force in expressions of outrage over the rise of Hitlerism. Indeed, it was *Dr. Abraham Coralnick* (1883-1937), a feature writer of *Der Tog*, who initially advocated a boycott of Nazi Germany.

In this vein, but at an earlier time, *Dos Tageblat* (The Daily Bulletin) printed a special English page from September 1897 to 1907 and reintroduced it in 1914. The more difficult words were translated and explained in Yiddish thus enabling immigrant readers to acquire and augment their English vocabulary.

Der Tog, which first appeared in November 1914 and amalgamated with *Di Warheit* (The Truth) in 1919, started with a weekly English supplement and a subsequent editorial column on the front page. This format was followed until the terminal date of publication, December 1971. All Yiddish newspapers, at one time or another, printed special articles dealing with American history, government, geography, education and politics. Descriptions of continental natural beauty were a regular feature. Information concerning naturalization, including the arrival dates of ships, and location of special courts, was freely given in response to queries by readers who proposed to take out their first or second citizenship papers. Special correspondents reported on events of national importance and projected legislation in Congress, as well as state and municipal legislatures.

The underlying purpose of presenting this material, along with the English supplements and columns, was twofold: first to create a positive attitude on the part of immigrant parents by stimulating and cultivating wholesome Jewish interests and, second, to help adult readers acquire a more substantial knowledge of America, its language and culture, thereby hastening the acculturation process. An effective attempt at accelerating linguistic integration was made by the *Forward* during the latter part of 1920 into early 1921 – a peak period of Jewish arrival. It printed a series of lessons (prepared by *Alexander Harkavy*) designed to meet the needs of those who could neither speak nor read English.

The press left an ineradicable impress, because it offered newcomers a guide to the new world, helped them understand strange issues, and interpreted questions in a trustworthy manner. Above all, it served as an Americanizing agency. The daily editions and weekly supplements published stories, poetry, exhortative articles, as well as advice to the lovelorn, the misunderstood parent and the heartsick. As free citizens they were drawn into a multitude of new activities. The press was meaningful insofar as it furthered their participation.

It was at this point in time that Samuel Niger began to make his unique contribution to this remarkable epoch in Jewish history.

Chapter III

Niger's creative personality is a conglomerate of paradoxical components. He had a passionate love for his people yet could easily be drawn into petty caviling. His general erudition, ranging from Plato to Freud was enormous, but his literary tastes were quite parochial. He was, perhaps, more comfortable as an analyst of, and a commentator on, public events, yet almost all the books he published were confined to literary criticism. He was essentially a pragmatist who found great difficulty in husbanding his talents. Consequently, there was a marked disproportion between the number of serious studies devoted to criticism and the thousands of articles pressed into a journalistic framework, thus making it almost impossible to attempt a sequential analysis of the various topics which attracted his attention. He stepped into the arena of divergent opinion with great alacrity, even though he considered the world of polemics ancillary to his primary calling as a critic. Although he could annihilate a writer or poet with great aplomb, he could not appreciate, or become reconciled to, the hostility shown by victims of his frequently devastating criticism.

In order to understand Niger more clearly, one must view his character and creative talents in terms of his ideological conception of the historicity and nationalistic configuration of Jewish life. Many noble dimensions of Jewish history and culture, which he viewed as an entity, were fused within him so that, in effect, he straddled both major focii of Jewish settlement in the 20th century, United States and Eastern Europe, and thus acted as a bridge between reality and fiction; the present and the past; new ideas and antiquated ones; secularism and traditionalism; Yiddish and Hebrew; the State of Israel and the Diaspora.

Although he may have been a synthesis of these several elements, he was, nonetheless, a decisive partisan. He usually took a definitive stance on an issue out of profound conviction, he maintained. Thus he stood against most Zionists by advocating a bi-national state in Palestine. Interestingly enough, he presumed his position to be intrinsically valid because he considered himself to be more objective than most people. A careful study of his writings might lead to the conclusion, however, that his partisanship was often multidimensional. He was a realist whose pragmatism was based on historic authenticity. His life in the present was an extrapolation of the creative past. He was attracted by the elegant and subtle which were often juxtaposed to the harsh and real. He lived as a secularist while constantly harking back to traditionalism. He helped nurture the tree of Yiddish whose true, deep roots are Hebrew. Finally, he realized that he was living in the Diaspora, with *Eretz Yisroel* in the ever present background.

Niger spent the greater portion of his intellectual life attempting to reconcile divergent positions which he had polarized over a period of years. As a young man he tended toward territorialism. Later on, he became an ardent Socialist-Labor Zionist. In his more mature years, under the impact of the 1929 riots in Palestine and the impending doom he foresaw with the rise of Hitler, he concluded that there must be a Jewish State in Palestine, but in a bi-national setting. With all the obeisances he made in the direction of the historical cogency and political feasibility of Zionism, he could not fully reconcile the essential Jewish nationalism inherent in this concept with his life-long penchant for internationalism, the outcome of his socialist-secularistic outlook. Also, with remarkable prescience, he feared the tendency of orthodox Jews to impose their religious outlook on the population of the Jewish State. For him, this would be tantamount to a theocracy, the very antithesis of classical Zionism. This might square with his affinity for Ahad-Ha'amism and the conclusion that only if the Jewish State is an integral part of the world at large can it have viability and validity.

He was obsessed with the importance of intellectual integrity and, therefore, made short shrift of writers and lecturers who lacked the courage and strength to take a stand on an issue and delineate clearly the premises of their contentions. Yet ofttimes he was equally as guilty of this transgression as those whom he castigated when he adopted a patronizing attitude towards "the masses" while dealing with a controversial matter.

Thus his commentaries on American Jewish life, for example, were probably a form of self-criticism, a reflection of an innate ambivalence. On the one hand he believed that the American Jew had a positive cultural future. On the other, he looked back nostalgically to Jewish life in Eastern Europe while failing to grasp the impracticability of transplanting it to the New World. He, therefore, chastised the secularist Yiddishists for their lack of Jewish content. At the same time he turned on the traditionalists for accepting ritual as the ultimate while emptying Judaism of its eternal meanings. Nor did he spare the intellectuals who seemed to lack conviction and purpose as they indulged their propensity for formulating irrelevant ideas and concepts.

He had deep affection for his people with particular compassion for "the common man." He would never chasten the masses nor hold them responsible for deficiencies of the group. Instead, he constantly faulted leaders and intellectual frontrunners because, he contended, they had a solemn obligation to set the scholarly and cultural norms that normally enhance the life-style of a people.

Nevertheless, throughout his entire creative career, Niger "the *Litvak*" (the Lithuanian) could not (nor did he so desire) rid himself of the illusion that he belonged to the East European Jewish aristocracy of the intellect. He would speak lovingly, as well as patronizingly, of humble Hasidim. But while lashing out at the intelligentsia, he never abandoned fully the tone of respect which underlay his sometimes vociferous objections to their stance. Thus when he criticized secularists, Yiddishists, labor leaders or even nationalists, he was simply baring his soul and revealing the frustrations that gripped him to the end of his days. He would have liked to see a Jewish Nobel Laureate for literature so recognized by virtue of his essentially Jewish creativity. He yearned to expand the framework of his own critical writing so that its influence would reach beyond the Yiddish reading and speaking world, yet he never undertook a work which might appeal to a broader audience. Perhaps, he rationalized, his time was too limited.

Ideologically he dreamed about a Jewish community (particularly in the United States) which would be a felicitous fusion of secularism with traditionalism; Jewish content in "worldly" forms; an intellectual climate wherein Jewish values would set the criteria for enhancing the human condition. This inner conflict is further attestation of the ambivalence under which he labored. He was the ultimate realist who struggled with life's realities. One might conclude that in criticizing others he really called attention to his own shortcomings. He probably did not realize that while inveighing against a particular person, concept or ideology, he actually revealed his own inadequacies.

Niger thought of himself as a true son of Israel who felt comfortable in a cosmopolitan era. Consequently, throughout most of his creative career he grappled with the juxtaposition of form and content. On those rare occasions when he attended religious services he preferred a "shul" to a synagogue and a "chazen" to a cantor. Withal that he was quite consistent. He kept very few of the six hundred and thirteen precepts incumbent upon an orthodox Jew because he defined secularism as the elimination of ritual observance. Although he never fully came to terms with this paradox he could not restrain himself from blaming contemporary "freethinkers" who rejected the obligations of religious practice but did not hesitate to participate in the more colorful externalities of Jewish life.

Although personally eschewing orthodoxy, Niger equated secularism with Reform Judaism because, he contended, both placed the emphasis on external form rather than intrinsic content. He maintained, further, that a major deficiency of the Reform movement lay in the tendency to revise or eliminate rituals no longer consonant with the times. Here, too, his conscious attitude and subconscious penchant for traditionalism came into open conflict. He was convinced that modern Jewish life was becoming increasingly secularized and courted the danger of fading into insignificance. He who made elegance of style a cardinal principle of literary creativity decried the fact that his contemporary, secularist friends made a fetish of forms instead of developing and fleshing out the concepts of secularism as applied to the Jewish people, resulting in the evaporation of many traditional Jewish values.

He never represented himself as a philosopher, nor did he create a crystallized system of thought. This might explain his lack of essentially philosophic works. Thus the astringent pragmatism of *Halachah* (rabbinic law) intrigued him so that he considered rabbinic Judaism the epitome of intellectual egalitarianism, the product of the Sages' unfettered interchange of ideas and concepts, down through the ages. Ritual observance was more a cultural/social phenomenon than a response to a religious or divine ordinance. This attitude coincided neatly with his conviction that a good Jew is a learned one, but not necessarily pious.

He vigorously resisted the blandishments of a precisely formulated ideology whose lack of openness he equated with a form of cultural stultification. As an intellectual, he insisted upon complete freedom of expression, whether the subject be Socialism, Zionism or religion. As for Judaism, he maintained it was a composite of values, concepts, ideas, aspirations and forms. The longevity of the Jewish people would be a direct function of the longing for compatibility.

The self-conscious nostalgia for Jewish tradition was an ever-present component in the various issues to which he addressed himself. For him, language was merely the vessel in which thoughts are contained; the golden thread that runs through a people's historic and cultural continuum. Thus, he was the secularist Yiddishist who insisted that a command of elegant Yiddish is impossible without an extensive knowledge of Hebrew. He maintained (particularly during the 1920s) that secular Judaism, devoid of the kaleidoscopic colorfulness of Jewish tradition, is a hollow shell. Nevertheless, he did nothing to introduce Hebraic studies into the curricula of either the *Sholem Aleichem* or *Arbeiter Ring* Yiddish school systems in which he played an important role.

Niger realized that New York, in the inter-War years, was neither Vilna nor Warsaw. The cultural heights to which these communities scaled and the use of Yiddish as the lingua franca reflected their proximity to the traditionalist centers whence they sprang and the audiences to whom they turned. Still, he could not reconcile himself to the inevitable, that it would be impossible to have the best of both worlds simultaneously. He recognized the many deficiencies of East European life and admitted that not every Jew was a scholar nor did he have an unshakable faith in God and love of His people. They were often petty, snide and even vicious. There were those who confused means with ends. Others sacrificed principles in order to achieve practical objectives. Nevertheless, he vainly hoped that the millions of immigrants who flocked to the New World would be able to live materially as never before while enjoying the view from the cultural Olympus which they will have transposed from their former home. Yet even as the realist overshadowed the mystic in him, he never referred to the seamy side of life in Eastern Europe while upbraiding American Jews for their apathy and disinterestedness.

This mild-mannered, soft-spoken, cultivated human being was also capable of crusading intensity. He was embroiled in a series of confrontations and recriminations most of his life. Some, like the advocacy of a bi-national state in Palestine, he faced head-on. Others, like contentious poets and authors, he attempted to shrug off. Those considered beneath his dignity were simply ignored. But he never retreated. He consistently maintained that his different positions and attitudes were invariably predicated on principle and conviction, so that even in the heat of controversy he never abandoned his standards of excellence and partiality for elegance.

Niger the mystic loved his people with a quiet, subtle reverence and, very much like a parent, grieved over the inadequacies as he was exhilarated by the achievements of his children. However, Niger the pragmatist understood that cruel history had drafted a perverse scenario for the Jew. Does this clarify the dilemma of "whom the Lord loveth He chastiseth"? (Prov. 3:12) In an exceedingly small measure, such was the tone Niger adopted towards his people.

Chapter IV

From the start of his career Niger attracted readers' attention not only by the seriousness of approach to issues nor the innovativeness of thought, but by the uniqueness of style, the so-called "Niger touch." It appears that in his early works he revelled in the concepts and inventions of the language, particularly with regard to the manipulation of antitheses. This may have led several aspiring young writers to engage in a form of gracious, linguistic playfulness which pointed up the virtuosity and limitless possibilities of Yiddish.

Niger's major contribution to Yiddish literature lay in the field of literary criticism. He readily appreciated the fact that in the world of artistic creativity there are many elements, in addition to one's roots, which shape the artist, i.e. environment; folk traditions and mores; current ideas; values that influence him; fleeting, mercurial flights of fantasy; the overarching ambition to carve a niche in history. Niger's unusual powers of discernment enabled him to distinguish clearly between the positive and negative qualities of the author at hand because, he maintained, the writer is at his best when he is true to himself, and expresses the innermost wranglings of his soul. On the other hand, he is at his worst when his work reflects peripheral pressures and momentary or superficial tendencies, despite the fact that such pieces sometimes have a glistening patina.

Thus the artist should be introspective and learn to assess the conditions, potentialities and, what is more, the outer limits of his abilities within which he must confine himself. Likewise, the skeptical researcher should draw guidelines for sorting out those works that might become an integral part of the literature from those which should be relegated to the oblivion of mediocrity.

Niger was a literary historian as well as critic and researcher. In a series of monographs and articles he demonstrated that modern Yiddish creativity was not an ephemeral caprice of history nor a prop to sustain a passing need. On the contrary. The people's entire cultural development is the product of a generations-long yearning and spiritual rootedness. This, perhaps, explains his incisive, probing attention to political issues and involvement in polemics which date from the turn of the century when he was drawn to the Socialist-Zionist movement and became aware of the social justice dimensions of the Jewish renaissance.

The matter of bi-lingualism in Jewish literature – a people with two cultures – occupied Niger, with consuming interest, most of his life. He understood that the propensity for accommodating to host cultures is characteristic of the Diaspora. At the onset of the *Haskalah* (Enlightenment), *Maskilim* (Enlighteners: maskil=singular) naively defined emancipation as the desire to know one's neighbor at close range. However, as the 19th century passed into the 20th, a pattern emerged whereby Jews either assimilated into the contiguous culture, as was the case with the intelligentsia, or it remained a *terra incognita* for the majority because of their insularity. There were also those Jews who ignored the language and life-style of the country and simultaneously allowed their Jewish background to evaporate.

It should be noted that in the course of its millenial dispersion, the Jewish people lived more with its past than its future. The national present was of interest essentially in a negative sense inasmuch as the Jew was concerned primarily with persecution and the need for self-preservation. Hence, late in the 19th century, their national consciousness was aroused, leading some to the conclusion that only autoemancipation can open the gates to a happy tomorrow. Even then, Jewish organizations and activists set their sights towards a future shrouded in amorphous notions. Zionists were convinced they were on the threshold of a Jewish State and would be able to abandon the oppressive Diaspora. Bundists maintained that a successful revolution would automatically obviate the Jewish question. Both camps studiously ignored the national and cultural present.

Nevertheless, Niger suggested that the present could not be ignored. It is the bridge between the past and the future; the laboratory of reality in which the soul of a people incorporates the content and experiences of life. The present requires that one relate to it not only with attentiveness, but with love. One should serve it, listen to its demands and fulfill all its requests. A people unaffected by its present does not deserve to be referred to as such, because the term implies a living organism. Those, on the other hand, whose totality of existence and reality rely only on hopes for the future, constantly live in the shadow of destruction.

In this sense, many Jewish intellectuals, during the first two decades of the 20th century, viewed their compatriots' creativity as mainly Yiddish oriented and of abysmally low quality. They stood removed from the structure of Yiddish letters and considered it a ramshackle hut. These people dreamt only of the future but neglected the salient fact that Jewish culture, like every other, has a past, a history, and is the product of an organically developed environment. A culture can blossom only if it strikes deep roots.

Y.L. Peretz (1852-1915) once pointed out that the language underwent a series of tranformations until it became the Yiddish known in his day, allowing that the Jewish people simply could not refer to it otherwise. It was the tongue in which it lived out the totality of its life; a language which it assimilated, changing form and structure while pouring its soul into it; its sorrow, anger, longing, hopes, and prayers. Half a millenium before, the Jew took a strange shoot, implanted it in his heart and watered it with his tears and blood. What flowered was Yiddish.

He further suggested that all modern languages, without exception, stem from a variety of ancient linguistic elements – and that includes Yiddish. It remained a *jargon* only for those who did not truly identify with their people and could neither read nor write it. Hebrew ties us to our past, but Yiddish is the bond with the present. Without Yiddish there could not be any vibrant Jewish life.

In agreement, *Chaim Zhitlovsky* (1865-1943) maintained that a meaningful aspect of Jewish national life may be called the "cultural revolution." This implied a critical evaluation of all those cultural values by which the Jewish people had lived, ultimately resulting not only in liberation from religious norms, but also in a rejection of the Hebraic parameters in which higher Jewish culture had existed. He held that the religious framework of its cultural life had compartmentalized the Jewish people into two categories – "the learned" and "the ignoramuses." It erected a barrier between the intelligentsia and the common man. The cultural revolution, which at that time was characterized by Yiddishism, razed that bar, heightened the desire for educational egalitarianism, and helped create an atmosphere whereby the more worldly classes would be able to identify with their people and would not have to seek their intellectual fortunes among strangers.

For Zhitlovsky, Yiddishism was the most radical expression of the progressive-nationalistic school of thought. It emerged as an amorphous, anonymous, mass process, which from the outset did not understand how deep were the life needs which called it forth; how great the forces which propelled it; how noble the objectives to which it aspired. It was perhaps the only movement among the Jewish people which had come to complete maturity; to the self-assessment of its own strength and significance. He was convinced that Yiddish was the soul of that part of the Jewish people which strove toward a progressive life. As long as Yiddish would endure there could be no doubt about the viability of the Jewish people. The struggle for Yiddish, therefore, was a matter of life and death for its very existence and humanistic development.

Contrariwise, in order to emphasize the superficiality of Yiddish culture, Hebraists, particularly during the first two decades of the 20th century, pointed to giants of Hebraic and rabbinic learning like *Moses Maimonides* (1135-1204), *Solomon Ibn Gebirol* (1020-1057), and *Yehudah Halevi* (1075-1141). They further contended that Yiddish was inherently incapable of giving expression to an *Isaiah, Saadia Gaon* (882-942), *Baruch Spinoza* (1632-1677) or *Hermann Cohen* (1842-1918). According to *Ahad Ha'am* (1856-1927), therefore, one must reach the conclusion that only Hebrew literature is truly the national literature of the Jewish people, despite the fact that in recent times it had been sadly impoverished.

Leading Yiddishists, on the other hand, asserted that the *selbsthass* of the 1920s stemmed from ambivalence and insecurity, because intellectuals failed to concede that Yiddish had been the vehicle of Jewish expression for several generations. It uncovered the very soul of the Jew. It was as intimate a part of the Jewish people as a language can be. Yiddish was the tongue of the masses. Poets, politicians and propagandists realized that it was the only means whereby they could reach the larger portion of Jews around the world. It was the mortar which bound them together everywhere, even though its humble, sustaining qualities do not characterize materials from which enduring art works are fashioned (perhaps this accounted for the lack of great Jewish creativity, according to criteria of the intelligentsia.) Yiddish, by virtue of its homeliness could describe only the love and hates, aspirations and frustrations of the Jewish people. It might not possess the stentorian tones of other languages, yet it spoke in a mode which resonated. Could it be that these intellectuals sought a pinnacle or two to preen themselves in the presence of their non-Jewish neighbors, with whom they felt uncomfortable? It was also possible that they found Yiddish culture so penetrating and introspective that they feared it might reveal faults in their own outlook.

Extreme Yiddishists enjoyed attacking Hebraists just as confirmed Hebraists relished prophesying the imminent demise of Yiddish. Instead of developing Jewish cultural forms – each to his specific *genre* and *milieu* – and protecting themselves from lurking external and internal dangers, each group attacked the other and turned the language confrontation into an embittered and entrenched, partisan struggle. Among others, *Abraham Menes* (1897-1969) insisted that Hebrew always had priority, because from ancient times it had been *the* literary instrumentality. Ironically, during the *Haskalah* it became the lingua franca of secularists, yet never found its way to the average reader, thus enabling the intellectual to seek a release from the problem of bi-lingualism. Hebraists sought to transform the literary language into the vernacular, whereas Yiddishists hoped to convert the folk language into a medium of modern cultural renaissance. Both ventures produced extraordinary results.

Hebraists adopted a mundane orientation as opposed to Yiddishists who considered it their responsibility to heighten the importance of the language in the eyes of the populace. As both camps delved into the historical development of Yiddish it became increasingly apparent that Yiddish has a respectable geneaology within the framework of Jewish history.

This *kulturkampf* took on such a partisan cast because of the crushing disappointment in the first Russian Revolution (1905). The remnant of the Socialist intelligentsia, which remained loyal to the Bundist and Socialist-Zionist movements, became steeped in cultural activities. Zionist youth likewise devoted more of their energy and attention to cultural work than to political endeavor. The compulsiveness and embitterment of previous political jousts were transferred to the cultural and linguistic arenas. Thus the more moderate and determined radicals often resorted to epithets in an attempt to annihilate their opponents, when all else seemed to fail. They would sometimes pontificate in grandiose phrases which, when carefully examined, turned out to be quite meaningless.

There was a more objective factor which intensified this clash. Despite the proliferation of Zionism among the Jewish masses during the inter-War years, Yiddish finally became the dominant means of communication. As a result of great literary and artistic strides in Europe to which an elite group within the Jewish community was exposed, new trends and forces affected its social structure. The preponderance of Jews, urbanized, proletarian, and secularistic, were led by revolutionaries with little education and a literacy limited to Yiddish.

Several leading commentators of the time claimed that much of the internal tension was created by old foes of Yiddish – the assimilationists – who hoped the Jewish people would gradually disappear. Another source of this intramural strife stemmed from those who sought to bring about the "Zionist Messiah" and considered Yiddish to be insufficiently Jewish. On the other hand, Yiddishists did not aspire to create something new as did the Hebraists who aimed to resurrect the Hebrew language. One did not have to make Yiddish vital, to implant it or make it stronger, because it was indeed very much alive and deeply ingrained in Jewish culture. While no one was interested in uprooting Hebrew, the most integral element of Jewish religious and literary life, it was assumed that the Yiddishists possessed the capacity to project into the future very much as did the *maskilim* of the 19th century with regard to Jewish learning. They could actually delineate the role they foresaw for Yiddish and its significance for the Jewish people. In effect, they wanted the people to glean from its language that which could be creative and productive, thus enhancing their self-respect and posture.

Conversely, the Jewish intelligentsia preferred to speak Russian. Originally they attempted to teach it to the Jewish working masses, hoping to raise them to the level of Russian revolutionary notables. This may have been feasible had they confined their propagandistic efforts to narrow circles. However, when they went over from propaganda to agitation and broadened the base of operations, the Socialist leadership was compelled to express itself in Yiddish, even if it meant learning the language. More important was the fact that inasmuch as these revolutionaries campaigned for the rights of the Jewish proletariat, they likewise sought recognition for its language, since the struggle for civil rights was transmuted into one for national equality and Jewish cultural autonomy.

It followed, therefore, that if by the 1920s Yiddish had in fact become the national language of the Jewish people, its social life would be confined within the parameters of Yiddish culture, thereby eliminating the distinction between the intelligentsia and the masses. That implied that the former would tend to become more folksy and, perforce, employ the vernacular of the people. In effect the language will have evolved into a meaningful element, a self-contained cultural ingredient.

Consequently, its importance increased, both ideologically and practically, with regard to the press, literature, and theater. But this gave rise to countervailing tendencies which manifested themselves in an interesting manner. As the Jewish masses became more self-conscious and energetic, Yiddish culture assumed an increasingly central role. It became the instrumentality and outlet for their spiritual development and social activity. Conversely, as Yiddish culture was enriched, its influence on the public was heightened.

Max Weinreich (1894-1969), the eminent historian of the Yiddish language, pointed out that it evolved rather gradually as a definitive dimension in Jewish life. It first appeared as glosses in Holy Writ and as liturgical translations. Ultimately, it took on a more literary form. Well into the 20th century Jewish merchants customarily drafted commercial documents in Hebrew, as best as they could. However, when they met, all transactions were conducted in Yiddish. The same applied to rabbinic scholars. Their responsa were written in Hebrew, whereas in conversation they reverted to Yiddish, regardless of how intricate the issue at hand. Not only mundane aspects of living, but also all oral religious learning was conducted in Yiddish, from the first verse of Leviticus which the young child learned by rote, to complex analysis of the more esoteric tractates of Talmud. Thus there developed a symbiotic relationship between the two languages.

It should be noted that Socialism was not the sole force in the Jewish cultural renaissance. Just as the movement provided Jewish laborers with a sense of pride, and encouraged the satisfaction of their intellectual hunger in the humanitarian sense, Zionism aroused their nationalistic consciousness. Not only Socialists resorted to Yiddish as the medium for spreading their ideological programs, but Zionists as well. Thus within two decades after the *First Language Conference in Czernowitz* (1908), and because of variegated trends within the Jewish world at the time, there emerged, in addition to a Yiddish labor press and literature, a host of informational and belletristic works.

The newly found cultural and social vigor of the 1920s sharpened the truculence and aggressiveness of Yiddishists, and caused great consternation in the distraught Hebraist camp, because they sensed that behind Yiddishism as an ideology there stood Yiddish as a new, purely objective dynamic, a tongue which proliferated into every walk of life and assumed increasing centrality in modern Jewish cultural activity.

Chaim Nahman Bialik (1873-1934) archly remarked that the language question created a great deal of tension within the Jewish people. It polluted the intellectual air and became a stumbling block in the path of their social, literary, and national creativity. There seemed to be more personal and partisan ambition involved than a search for truth.

In the final analysis, language in the life of a people is essentially an historic phenomenon, limited by rigid rules which determine both its rootedness and uprootedness.

He proceeded on the premise that a normal people has one language because it is usually too involved to be interested in multi-lingualism. He referred to the psycho-philosophic debate which posited that while, on the one hand, multi-lingualism enriches the person, on the other, it simply confuses and impoverishes him. It is also difficult to determine whether through the acquisition of another language one also develops fresh concepts or merely adds a ballast of new words. The sad reality is that the Jewish people, whose national status has been abysmally abnormal, has trundled around with several languages – by necessity rather than choice.

Characteristically, Bialik offered an interesting insight into the method whereby Jews solved the language question educationally. The essential part of the school curriculum was the Hebrew book. All components, including the non-religious ones, were studied in Hebrew. It is incorrect to assume that the Jewish school was entirely religion oriented. He pointed out that some three hundred years ago there were schools in the Diaspora where students read philosophy, astronomy, mathematics and other disciplines. Obviously, these studies were religion biased, as was science generally at that time. The vernacular was used as a means of explanation, but never as curricular core. As soon as a student reached the point where he could deal with original texts, the vernacular was dispensed with. Even mature scholars, as they studied Talmud, would translate parts of the text into Yiddish, even though they certainly understood the original. This merely indicated a reflexive return to the national language. By translating the Hebrew into Yiddish, it was refreshed and revitalized through the intimacy with a living tongue. Into the Hebrew was poured the essence and taste of Yiddish, thus preventing the Hebrew from becoming a synthetic, or even a dead, literary language, like Latin.

The chasm widened after World War I. In the wake of this tragic upheaval millions of Jews were uprooted and fled from homesteads they had occupied for generations. Many were dislocated spiritually as well as physically. Children who were unable to attend school could respond to neither the spirit of a cultural continuum nor the burden of a bi-lingual, multifaceted culture. One language and literature was more than most could contend with. In the stress of post-War migrations large segments of the Jewish people wandered about as if in a stupor. When finally they found a haven, they had to exert themselves to the limit in order to adjust to the unknown, threatening geographic, political, and economic conditions. Understandably, they took the path of least resistance in cultural matters. With regard to Jewish education, literature, etc., this meant mono-lingualism.

Two Jewish communities of a new sort arose after World War I. Both concluded that it would be impossible to conduct their cultural life on the traditional premise of bi-lingualism. One was the *Yishuv* in Palestine; the other, Sovietized Jewish settlement in Russia. In each of these lands the Jewish leadership had its own ends and means. In Palestine the end was national revolutionary. The means: social control. In Russia the aim was social revolutionary, via the proletarian dictatorship. Ironically, the one point of agreement between these two divergent philosophies was the conscious and organized opposition to the Jewish tradition of bi-lingualism. In the developing *Yishuv* they attempted to minimize or totally eliminate the influence of Yiddish as an educational and cultural factor. In Soviet Russia they excluded Hebrew from the Jewish educational system and cultural life. In the one land they hoped to erase the image of the Diaspora Jew in the present, and in the other they were no longer interested in a "benighted" past.

For the first time the Jewish people was no longer confronted by the question of Hebrew *and* Yiddish, but by the dichotomy of either Hebrew *or* Yiddish. There existed the danger, therefore, that litterateurs and Jewish historians would ignore the relationship between Hebrew and Yiddish, and what is more depressing, the bond of Yiddish to its Hebraic heritage.

Perpetuating the wall of antagonism spelled impoverishment for both camps. For Hebrew literature this meant severing deeply sunk roots; for Yiddish, the loss of branches which were vital and fruitful. This was particularly perilous in the post-War era when the language of the host country became a dominating factor, forceful enough to eclipse both Yiddish and Hebrew. Obviously, at such a moment it was incumbent upon all segments of the Jewish people to strengthen the unique forms of their national culture wherever they might be, and preserve its many treasures, both old and new.

Chapter V

While viewing the issue of bi-lingualism through the prism of history, Niger reached the conclusion that almost from the very beginning of the Jewish career it appears that one language did not suffice. The Bible included Aramaic sections in the books of Ezra and Daniel (note: some of the very earliest printed editions set the *Targum* [Aramaic] alongside the Masoretic text). Further on, he maintained, Talmud stands as a monument to bi-lingualism, Aramaized Hebrew as found in the Mishna and Hebraized Aramaic in the Gemorra. Actually, by the turn of the millenium, Aramaic was the lingua franca in Palestine, while Hebrew the language of religion and spirituality.

Ironically, in this period of Hebrew-Aramaic bi-lingualism, there were almost no Aramaists who suggested that Hebrew be eliminated from Jewish life. However, there were Hebraists who failed to appreciate the need for another language despite the fact that Hebrew was no longer the vernacular. They contended that the appropriate tongue after Hebrew should be that of the establishment, Greek or Persian, but not Judaized Aramaic. A Talmudic passage reads: Rabbi stated: "why use the Syriac language in Eretz Yisrael [where] either the Holy Tongue or the Greek language [could be employed]? And Rabbi Jose said: why use the Aramaic language in Babylon [where] the Holy Tongue or the Persian language [could be used]"? (BK 82b) There were among the more moderate Hebraists those, who while not advocating the total abolition of Aramaic, warned against praying in the vernacular, because, they held, "Kings cannot understand it, they respond only to the Holy Tongue" (Sab. 12).

Nevertheless, in an extended course of time, and with persistent determination, Aramaic took its place beside Hebrew as a second literary medium. Thus, the *Jerusalem Talmud*, some of the *Midrashim* (Heb: interpretation of Biblical texts), and much of later rabbinic literature, were written in Hebraized Aramaic. Even *Josephus Flavius* (38-100?), in order to reach a wider audience, wrote "The Wars of the Jews" in Aramaic. Eventually it became the language of instruction in schools and yeshivas, as well as important documents, i.e. marriage contracts, bills of divorce and even some prayers.

As the use of Aramaic became more widespread, legends were recounted attesting to its importance. The tractate Sanhedrin states that "originally the Torah was given to the children of Israel in Hebrew characters and in the sacred [Hebrew] language; later, in the times of Ezra, the Torah was given in the *Ashurith* (Aramaic) script and language, leaving it for the *hedyoth* (common man)" (San. 21). Further on we are told that "according to Rav, Adam spoke Aramaic" (ibid. 35). This statement was undoubtedly meant to authenticate his descendents' use of the tongue as the vernacular and its increasing proliferation into various cultural aspects of the people's life. The Bible was translated several times into Aramaic leading to the tradition of *"shnayim mikra v'echad targum"* (In reviewing the weekly portion of the Pentateuch, one does so twice in Hebrew and once in Aramaic translation). Ultimately there was a confluence of the two languages, so that commentators on rabbinic literature would frequently, unconsciously use both Hebrew and Aramaic interchangeably.

Poetry in all forms was usually written in Hebrew, whereas Kabbalists preferred Aramaic (The Zohar), which they sanctified equally with the Holy Tongue. Consequently, Aramaic transcended its original geographic boundaries, very much like Yiddish-German, which took root in lands where no one knew German. Jews spoke and wrote Aramaic in far-flung places where it was unknown. Ironically, thanks to the Jew, Aramaic is still alive, as it resonates in the synagogue and yeshiva. Modern Hebrew includes innumerable Aramaic terms, as it does Yiddish idioms and expressions.

Aramaic remained a literary medium long after it ceased being spoken, inasmuch as, in some instances, it was combined with Hebrew, and in other cases acquired a sanctity of its own. Hence, Niger suggested, those who claim that it is unhistorical to place Yiddish on an equal footing with Hebrew, in effect, deny the authenticity of history. It is likewise fallacious to presume the impossibility of creating a national literature based on a folk tongue. On the contrary. The Jewish cultural tradition has clearly demonstrated its compatibility with the growth and flowering of a literature in the language of the masses. Indeed, it has always been bi-lingual.

The emergence of Yiddish literature was hardly an innovative phenomenon. The Talmud had already produced an oral tongue based on the multi-generational experience of Aramaic, a fact known to most of those engaged in fashioning a literature in the folk language. On the one hand this was necessitated by the need to address some practical religious issues, and on the other to justify generating works in that *gross*, mundane language.

Returning to the tradition of reviewing the weekly Torah portion "twice in Hebrew and once in Aramaic," the practicability of the custom, in its time, should be borne in mind. The practice was carried forward long after Jews ceased speaking Aramaic, by then a synonym for a language no one understood. Like so many other religious observances, it became obsolete, without any rationale for continuing. Originally, it evolved as an aid to understanding the Hebrew text while using Aramaic as the vernacular. However, as Jews started speaking other tongues, Aramaic became as incomprehensible as Hebrew, rendering this formality meaningless because they understood neither the original nor the translation. Many leading rabbis, disturbed by this development, came to the conclusion that the Aramaic Targum had to give way to the *Yiddish Teitch* (translation), thereby bringing the Jewish people into a new cultural era.

Since the early sixteenth century hundreds of books have been published in a bi-lingual format, but with a new feature. The Targum was replaced by *Ivre-Teitch* – a simplistic, pedantic, Yiddish translation of the Hebrew. This literary parallelism continued into modern times.

Thus bi-lingualism became an established fact, a tradition; not only in the *Teitch-Chumash* (Pentateuch), *Musar* (moralizing) tracts, prayers and supplications, but in the Haskalah pamphlets of the 19th century as well. These displayed a close partnership between Yiddish and Hebrew by inserting Hebrew nomenclature, and sometimes entire sentences, into the Yiddish text. There were even those journals which printed Hebrew and

Yiddish articles side by side. Obviously, the writers had to be bi-lingual in order to produce such fare.

However, by the late 1930s Niger admitted that there was a definitive mono-lingual trend among Jews which manifested itself in the form of "100%" Hebraism on the one hand, and extreme Yiddishism on the other. The former strove to make Hebrew the exclusive medium of national creativity while the latter aimed to achieve the same for Yiddish. The result was that whereas a portion of the intelligentsia sought to minimize the significance and role of *jargon*, or the "ghetto tongue," another segment would have narrowed down Hebrew, or even have eliminated it entirely, from Jewish life.

Both camps readily understood that should their respective aspirations become a reality, the Jewish people would suffer a grievous loss. Nevertheless, they were prepared to make the sacrifice because some believed it to be in the best interests of national unity while others held that the ensuing damage would be minimal. In any event, there were leaders, opinion makers, and commentators among the Hebraists who were ready to do without Yiddish in their cultural pursuits, as well as within the ranks of the Yiddishists, who felt they could survive without Hebrew.

* * *

At the close of the Middle Ages and the onset of the Renaissance, most nations of Europe, some sooner than others, were confronted with the problem of bi-lingualism. While Latin was the official, written tongue of the national components within the Roman empire, there began to emerge indigenous dialects which gradually evolved into mother tongues. Actually, the impetus came primarily from urbanites who bridged the culturally disparate sections of the population, the cultivated and the provincials. Withal that, for a considerable time, there was almost no contact between the two, because the one was the language of literature, learning and prayer, whereas the other was undeveloped, oral, and the lyrics for ballads.

Under the impact of urbanization, spreading commerce and the invention of printing, the folk dialects – used exclusively for mundane communication – gradually, but increasingly, were heard in schools, religious life, literature and theater, thereby threatening the cultural dominion of Latin. Instead of remaining in their separate spheres as heretofore, the two languages sometimes overlapped or led to confrontations. Thus, as late as the 16th century, the dedicated English reformer, William Tyndale, was persecuted and finally executed for persisting in translating the Bible into the vernacular. For an additional century it was generally accepted that any decent scientific work had to be written in Latin.

Throughout the long span of Roman hegemony over Europe, most of the nations experienced a tension between Latin – the established culture medium – and the folk dialect, an embryonic literary instrumentality. They underwent a cultural development similar to that of the Jewish people in Jesus' time, when Aramaic became the second literary language, alongside Hebrew.

Toward the end of the 15th century a "second language," *Ivre-Teitch* or Yiddish, began to take shape among Jews. This clearly reflected a development unfolding all over Europe which responded to the printer's art thereby making books cheaper and easier to distribute. More important, however, was the example set by their host communities where the vernacular was increasingly employed for religious and secular literary purposes. Likewise among Jews, *Ivre-Teitch* gradually assumed a distinctive role by the side of classical Hebrew.

Yiddish in its early stages, as in the case of all other folk tongues, was severely limited and incapable of dealing with complex scholarly matters. Hence non-Jews wrote in Latin, Jews in Hebrew-Aramaic. Yiddish, like the folk languages of their neighbors, was reserved for tales, chronicles, ballads, and popularization of "real" literature, thus pointing up the parallelism between Jewish cultural development and that of their surrounding societies.

However, in this instance there is a significant difference. For Jews everywhere, Hebrew represented a cultural heritage, a golden thread that ran through the fabric of their national history. Latin, on the other hand, was strange to most people in Europe at the time, except perhaps for Italy and the other Romance countries. Therefore the issue was not the exchange of a foreign language for an indigenous one, but the evolution of an own folk tongue to complement classical Hebrew, which, in the final analysis, belonged to every Jew, be he the scholar who struggled with a complex rabbinic text or a humble layman who prayed at the appointed times and recited appropriate blessings. Thus, in its early stages, Yiddish was little more than ancillary to the Hebrew.

Niger pointed out that perhaps the only similar instance of bi-lingualism would be the Italians. Latin for them was almost the same as Hebrew for Jews – the language of national tradition and culture. Initially, the folk dialect, which strove to became a literary language, was little more than a byproduct of its classical tongue. Yet the analogy between Latin-Italian and Hebrew-Yiddish is not entirely accurate. Under the impact of the Renaissance, and particularly such gifted luminaries as *Dante Alighieri* (1265-1321), *Francesco Petrarch* (1304-1374), and *Giovanni Boccaccio* (1313-1375), Italian rapidly became the national language in the artistic – if not scientific – sphere, and began to take the place of Latin. However, this process was not without travail. For a long time Italian was viewed condescendingly by the intelligentsia, including Petrarch who sneered that he chose to write his sonnets in "simple Italian" rather than "noble Latin."

In the case of the Jews, there was a marked difference. Not until the beginning of the 20th century did Yiddish have any pretensions at achieving parallelism with Hebrew. In fact, during the Enlightenment period, starting the middle of the 18th century, Hebrew gained a heightened status while Yiddish was deprecated, although in the atmosphere of humanism which prevailed at the time in Western Europe, interest in their respective folk tongues increased while preference for the classical languages diminished.

Niger sensed that the problem of bi-lingualism among Jews refused to go away because religion served to unite the people, whereas in other nations this function was fulfilled by land and language. Inasmuch as Hebrew has been the language of religious expression among Jews as well as the symbol of national unity, its place in the group consciousness is similar to that of the Italians with regard to Latin.

* * *

However, writing in two languages is another matter, including such closely intertwined tongues as Hebrew and Yiddish. Even the most gifted bi-lingual authors of the 20th century came to the conclusion that one can burnish and build in only one language at a time. It is impossible to play the same song on two instruments simultaneously.

Perhaps the only exceptions to this rule could be found among poets and thinkers of the Golden Age of Spain who wrote in both Hebrew and Arabic. This raises the question whether they might not have been more productive had they confined themselves exclusively to the language of their preference. Also, it should be borne in mind that they never employed the two languages for the same purpose, neither in their poetry nor the ethical tracts they produced. In each instance they chose the language considered most appropriate. Thus, Yehudah Halevi cast his poetry exclusively in Hebrew, whereas the philosophical/theological *Cuzari* was written in Arabic. Likwise the case of Solomon Ibn Gevirol who chose Hebrew as the vehicle for his poetry and Arabic for his philosophical and ethical works.

Moses Maimonides is the outstanding example of this literary ambivalence. Consequently, when he wrote the *Commentary On The Mishnah* in Arabic, which he undoubtedly intended should appear in Hebrew, he asked someone else to translate it. The same applied to Halevi's *Cuzari* (Kuzari), Bahya's *Hovoth Ha'lvavoth* (Duties of the Heart), and Ibn Gevirol's *Mekor Haim* (Fount of Life). Apparently, each of these commentators, while masters of both languages, concluded that a work should be created in the more appropriate tongue.

A similar situation obtained when Jewish literature passed from the Hebrew-Arabic phase into the Hebrew-Yiddish period. Some writers composed works in both languages, using Hebrew for one genre and Yiddish for a completely different sort. Invariably, one senses immediately the disparity in themes, motifs and format between those written in Hebrew and those in Yiddish. Bialik, for example, would never have considered writing his lyric *Mein Gorten* (My Garden) in Hebrew nor his *Megillat Aysh* (Scroll of Fire) in Yiddish. He had to do the latter in the tongue of the Prophets and the former – a humorous idyl about his grandmother's confiture – in the folk tongue.

Actually, it is easier to speak a foreign tongue than to write in it, because the written word demands a language that is an integral part of one's life-style, thought process, and experiences. It must speak while one is silently contemplative. It must come from the innermost recesses of the soul. There is only one such tongue for each author – in any event, for every different kind of work.

To be sure, there are a few exceptions that prove the rule. Hence, when Niger referred to Jewish literature as being bi-lingual he did not imply that most authors worked in both languages. Rather that they, like the myriads of Jewish readers, transferred quite naturally from one to the other. This might not have been the case with the American Jewish community, but it certainly applied to pre-World War II East European Jewry.

Chapter VI

Yiddish developed as the second literary language among Jews with greater difficulty than did Aramaic. However, from the beginning it played a discernible role in the religious and creative life of the people. Not only were popular non-Jewish songs sung, and tales recounted in Yiddish, but, more importantly, they began to craft religious hymns as well as books in the folk tongue. Many leading rabbis looked askance at this phenomenon, particularly when they discovered that religious law was being expounded in simple, understandable terms through this medium. Apparently they feared that if the common man/woman would become sufficiently informed, there would be no need for them to seek rabbinic judgements on religious matters. This interdiction applied not only to legal issues but also to liturgical ones. Grudgingly they relented in the case of special collections of "women's supplications."

Early in the 18th century, Aaron ben Samuel was roundly denounced by many rabbis because he wrote a prayer book in Yiddish. They viewed the work, and particularly the Foreword wherein he advocated that Jews should pray in Yiddish, as a piece of heresy and banned it.

But Ben Samuel was not alone in this contention. He was later to be joined by several great Hasidic Rabbis – the *Baal Shem Tov* (1700-1760), *R. Nahman of Bratzlav* (1772-1811), *R. Dov Ber of Lyadi* (1773-1827), and *R. Levi Yitzhok of Berditchev* (1740-1810). All shared the conviction that a devout Jew, who sincerely desires to pray and does not understand Hebrew, should be encouraged to do so in Yiddish, because prayer is the outpouring of the soul, and what purpose is served if the heart does not respond to the utterings of the lips. This attitude might explain, in part, the rapidity with which Hasidism, as a movement, swept over the Jewish communities of Europe.

There was the occasional, stubborn opponent of Yiddish who maintained that even ethical tracts should not be written in the vernacular, despite the warm reception accorded the translation of the classic *Menores Hamaor* (The Menorah of Light) in 1722. The author, *Moishe Frankfurt* (1672-1762), insisted that not only is such a work not heresy, but rather it is a *mitzvo* (a good deed) to enable one to study in a language which one comprehends. The precedent having been established, there followed a series of widely distributed *Musar* (morals) tracts, either written or translated into Yiddish, which exerted a signal influence on the life-style of Jews.

Obviously, some authors refused to be intimidated by opponents' arguments they considered groundless in light of Jewish history which, they maintained, has a tradition of bi-lingualism dating back to the Second Temple period. Thus, in addition to the many *Musar* tracts and *T'chinos* (set prayers – usually recited by women) the way was opened to a succession of religious works in Yiddish. Only the actual rabbinic texts, commentaries, and monographs were studied in Hebrew.

Thus the original *Teitch Chumash* (Pentateuch in Yiddish) evolved into the *Tz'enah Ur'ena* – a liturgical compilation embellished with a variety of commentaries, parables and homilies, that gained widespread popularity, particularly among women. It was characteristic of a range of Biblical works originally outlined and written in Yiddish, but definitely influenced by other Hebrew compendia (Talmud, Midrash), thereby retaining the flavor of the Hebrew while touching the reader in her folk tongue. It should be noted that by the 19th century the entire Bible had become available in Yiddish, as well as most of the *Aggadic* and *Musar* literature. Even though some works appeared only in Hebrew *or* Yiddish, this body of literature was essentially bi-lingual.

The same might be said for the secularist output of the Enlightenment period (18th-19th centuries). A substantial portion of old tales, chronicles, memoirs and travel brochures appeared in both languages, with the Yiddish patently influenced by the Hebrew. However, there was a vast difference between a Yiddish version of Aesop's fables and the *Ma'aseh Buch* (Story Book, first published in Basle, 1602), a compilation of some three hundred narratives taken from primarily Jewish sources. Thus began the development of an authentic literature that accurately reflected the aspirations and longings of the people.

* * *

The first works to be written (13th century) and then printed (16th century) in old Yiddish were so-called "Glossaries," which aimed to explain difficult words of the Bible. These were capped by *Reb Anshel of Cracow* (first half 16th century) who published, in 1534, a sort of concordance in Yiddish that listed them alphabetically, thereby making way for the first translation of the Pentateuch (Augsburg and Constanza, 1544). He set the pattern for most subsequent works in this early period of Yiddish literary endeavor when he stated on the title page "this book is a composite of two languages, the Holy Tongue and Ashkenasi," exemplifying, in effect, the close relationship between Hebrew and Yiddish-Teitch.

The first printed ethical tracts in Yiddish, *Musar un Hanhoge* (Ethics and Conduct) 1535, and *Safer Hamidos* (Book of Manners) 1542, are truly representative of both literatures. Some scholars suggest that the latter originally appeared in Yiddish and was then translated into Hebrew. Actually the reverse is correct. The Hebrew, written in the 15th century, was followed by a rather free Yiddish adaptation. These two works pioneered in the field of printed ethical literature in Yiddish which drew its sustenance from traditional Hebrew sources. Jewish life and culture in the Middle Ages, like that of their gentile neighbors, was entirely religion oriented, so that the fount of inspiration was Talmud, the primary example of the Hebrew-Aramaic tradition. No wonder, then, that the Bible, Talmud, Midrash, etc., served as points of departure for all subsequent literary creativity in Yiddish.

Since the *Halachic* (legalistic) phase of rabbinics proved to be much too complicated for "the common man," to say nothing of womenfolk, they derived enjoyment from the fascinating tales, parables, and wondrous imagery contained in these old books. Through the medium of the folk tongue, and while ignoring the scorn of scholars, they discovered *Aggadah*, the legendary side of Holy Writ, whose imaginative, educational and poetic aspects liberated them from the harsh strictures of *Halachah*. Thus *Aggadah* was lovingly embraced by the masses because it spoke to their hearts via a linguistic transformation into the *Ivre-Teitch*, while adhering to the Hebrew-Aramaic tradition.

Even such an unique example of religious literature in Yiddish, the *Veiberische T'chinos* (Women's Prayers), is deeply rooted in Hebrew liturgy. Undoubtedly, the many prayers composed in Hebrew and Aramaic by the Safed school of *Kabbalists* (mystics), as well as others, exerted a marked influence on the evolving *T'chinos*. Inasmuch as prayer represented the deepest of mysteries, and the canonized *Siddur* (Prayer Book) did not suffice, or was beyond them, they created a body of poetic and heartfelt supplications which expressed their pathos and fierce love of God. These became models for the many Yiddish *T'chinos* that followed.

In the course of some five hundred years, from the Middle Ages to the Enlightenment, there existed a close relationship between Hebrew and Yiddish. Letters, proclamations, rabbinic decisions, were frequently written in a combination of both, thereby reflecting the ingrained ambivalence toward the two cultures.

By way of a classic illustration, Niger suggested that the winds of change in the realm of Hebrew/Yiddish literature were most manifest in *Kabbalah* (Mysticism) and *Musar* (ethics/moral admonition) – primarily in the 16th and 17th centuries – as well as Hasidism and Enlightenment in the 18th and 19th centuries.

Kabbalah had a distinctive impact on both Hebrew and Yiddish writings. In fact "it freed the fantasy and gave wing to the spirit." There emerged a rather extensive body of literature in both languages that was saturated with the vital force of Jewish mysticism and which had its own bible – the *Zohar* (splendor). Ultimately, all these works appeared in Yiddish, thereby becoming available to a broader segment of the population.

The first Yiddish translator of the *Zohar* was a Rabbi in Poland, *R. Zelig the Kabbalist*. Sadly, he died before the work could appear. Shortly thereafter, one of his sons readied the manuscript for printing after receiving several testimonials from leading rabbis. However, this too was not to be. The Chmielnicki pogroms (1648) spread death and destruction throughout the countryside. Fortunately, the manuscript was spared and came into the hands of *Rabbi Zvi Hirsch Chotch* (c.1700), a grandson of Rabbi Zelig, who edited and published it under the title *Nahlas Zvi* (The Legacy of Zvi, Frankfurt-am-Main, 1711). In the Hebrew/Yiddish introduction he stated that Redemption can only come about through the *Zohar*, and since it is the prime source for Kabbalism it must be available in a Yiddish version. Incidentally, he further pointed out that the *Zohar* was written in Aramaic, the equivalent of Yiddish for then local Jewry. Therefore, inasmuch as the author of the *Zohar* had no compunctions about writing in the vernacular of his people, so should scholars of another time have no reservations with regard to reading holy texts in Yiddish.

Thus many Kabbalists were partial to both Aramaic and Yiddish. While referring to the prevailing interest in the subject, *Rabbi Moses Isserles* (1525-1572), the doyen of Ashkenazic rabbis, pointed out that "even the ordinary householder who does not know right from left, who wanders about in darkness, who cannot interpret a segment of the *Chumash* (Pentateuch) with *Rashi's* commentary, peruses Kabbalah." This accounts for the fact that the many mystical tracts, written in Hebrew/Aramaic, were usually translated into Yiddish.

However, it should be noted that since this literature developed along separate tracks it was aimed at two disparate groups. Inasmuch as the Hebrew/Aramaic versions attracted scholars, it was possible to expand the reader's horizons and probe extensively the many concepts and ideas imbedded in the texts. The Yiddish tracts, on the other hand, appealed to "the common man" for whom it sufficed to turn his attention to ethics/morals and fill his fantasy with the vagaries of life, colorful images and fascinating stories. Other than the "secrets" of Torah which were confined to the Hebrew/Aramaic editions, all the miraculous tales and imaginative interpretations were carried over into the Yiddish.

Whereas in the 16th and 17th centuries there was a symbiotic relationship between the *Kabbalah* and *Musar* movements, in the case of *Hasidism* and *Enlightenment* (18th and 19th centuries), there was only strife. However, with regard to language there existed a great similarity between the Kabbalist and his follower the Hasid, as well as the Musar writer and his heir, the "enlightener." They were all bi-lingual in their literary output.

Usually, works of complex delving into spiritual matters, in-depth research concerning Hasidism or the Enlightenment, as well as intricate discussions of Talmud and metaphysical philosophy of Kabbalah, were all written in Hebrew. Yiddish was reserved for legends, charming stories, parables and pamphlets. Thus, Hasidic and Enlightenment literature in

Yiddish was essentially that of *Aggadah*, belletristic, poetic, polemic, and consistently bi-lingual.

Such classics of Hasidic thought as *Toldos Yaakov Yosef* (Chronology of Jacob Josef – 1785) and the *Tania* (It is Taught – 1797) were written in Hebrew because of their scholarly or theoretical approach. However, *Shivhe Baal Shem Tov* (Praises of the Baal Shem Tov) and the tales of *R. Nahman of Bratzlav* appeared simultaneously in both languages (1815). The same applies to *Kahal Hasidim* (Congregation of Hasidim) and other compilations of fascinating stories which were meant to touch the emotions and fantasies of the folk. This could only be done through the language of the home and hearth – Yiddish.

The same applied to prayer – if one sought to express himself in a heartfelt manner and with deep concentration. Thus many Hasidic rabbis, primarily R. Nahman of Bratzlav, advised their followers to converse with God "in the mundane, spoken tongue (i.e. Yiddish) because one would have difficulty expressing himself freely in Hebrew. Also, since Yiddish is an integral part of daily living, it would be easier thereby to unburden one's self in the Divine presence." It therefore follows that if it is appropriate to converse with God in Yiddish, how much more so with one's fellow man.

The vernacular played a more important role among Hasidim, than, for example, Kabbalists, because it was a mass movement rather than a source of interest for individuals or small groups. As such, Hasidism had to rely on the folk language because its basic premise was devotion to God and belief in His wonders. Such depth of emotion, devout belief and boundless fantasy, could find release only via a living, spoken tongue. Understandably, Hasidism bequeathed to succeeding generations, on the one hand, Torah, exclusively in Hebrew, and on other, prayers, songs, parables and tales in Yiddish. No wonder, then, that the richest artistic legacy of the Hasidic world can be found in the tales of R. Nahman of Bratzlav, preserved in both Hebrew and Yiddish.

* * *

Opponents of Hasidism, the *Maskilim* ("enlighteners"; singular, *maskil*), paid scant attention to the phenomenon of Yiddish. For them, strictly speaking, the *Haskalah* (Enlightenment) was a phase of Hebrew literature in which writers broke away from traditional patterns to borrow the forms of secular European literature. But it was more than just a change in literary fashion; it was also an ideology. From the times of *Moses Mendelssohn* (1729-1786) – when he translated the Pentateuch into German to encourage Jews to abandon Yiddish, a language he detested as a debased form of German – to the 1880s, most of the *Maskilim* felt that Jews needed to modernize their life-style and absorb the new learning current outside the periphery of traditional Judaism. Like writers of the European-wide Enlightenment of the 18th century, the *Maskilim* were a loose group of social critics who called for an end to medievalism, praised the value of science and advocated various forms of social melioration. Above all, they preached reform of Jewish education, especially curtailment of the traditional Ashkenazic concentration on Talmudic studies. The *Haskalah* goal was a Jew who would embody a synthesis of Judaism and general culture, and would live up to the standards of common sense, tolerance and reasonableness, as espoused by universalistic humanitarianism.

Consequently it developed that in this atmosphere of Hebraism many writers rejected Yiddish and turned to the language of the land, German; then later, Russian and Polish. Some among them derided that "primitive German dialect." Others feared that *jargon*, as they referred to Yiddish, would separate Jews from the general population. If Jews are destined to be a bi-lingual people, they maintained, then let it be Hebrew and the vernacular of their host country.

Not all *Maskilim* shared this point of view. There were those who defended the necessity of a folk tongue and strived to preserve and cultivate it as an instrument of literary creativity. But this was a Sisyphusian effort. By the end of the 18th century the literary mode of western *Haskalah* had become completely Germanized, leading to the demise of most Hebrew publications.

From Germany and Galicia, the *Haskalah* was carried into Russia. Although there were already signs of an indigenous Russian Jewish modernization movement in late 18th century Lithuania, by the early 1850s the *Haskalah* had found its main home in Russia, where it entered its third and final phase. In Lithuania, European fiction and textbooks were translated into Hebrew, the first Hebrew novel was published (1854), and several significant Hebrew poets added a quality of personal lyricism previously missing in Hebrew verse. During the reign of the more liberal

Czar Alexander II, modern Hebrew weeklies appeared, and the *Society for the Promotion of Culture Among Jews of Russia* was established (1863). During the 1860s and 1870s a number of Hebrew writers who had rejected the decorative style of earlier *Maskilim* turned to literary and social criticism. After a hundred years of development, therefore, the *Haskalah* had introduced into Hebrew literature not only ideas of the 18th-century Enlightenment, but of almost every other European intellectual trend since then, including romanticism, philosophical idealism, and utopian socialism.

It should not be assumed that this led to a profusion of works and publications that inundated the Jewish community. On the contrary, their number was extremely limited. True, in the thrust toward modernism, most writers managed to put forward concepts and images garnered from literatures of the broad world. But they had to be constantly responsive to their targeted bi-lingual readership. Only thus could they have reached the majority of their brethren.

It would be impractical at this point to include a detailed survey of 19th century bi-lingual literature. Suffice to say that in none of the three most important periods of its literary history within this time frame – (a) the almost anachronistic *Musar* tracts (b) the spate of social and Socialist concepts, and (c) the burgeoning era of national renaissance – did *Haskalah* literature confine itself exclusively to one or the other of the two tongues. Some of the most distinguished writers of the Hebrew press consistently highlighted the importance of Yiddish. The reverse obtained in the Yiddish periodicals.

Chapter VII

The remarkably creative literary achievements of the second half of the 19th century ineluctably led to the *First Language Conference in Czernowitz*, a significant moment in the cultural development of the Jewish people as it crossed the threshold of the 20th century. For the first time the status of Yiddish was discussed in a forum representing a broad spectrum of parochial ideologies. The objective of the gathering was to determine the role Yiddish was to play in Jewish life.

Ironically, due to the inexperience of the Conference organizers, no accurate records were kept. Sources are limited to partisan reportage in newspapers and journals, reflected through the predilections of the respective writers. Consequently, minor issues were sometimes indiscriminately attacked, while elements of intrinsic motivation upon which the Conference was ostensibly predicated were frequently overlooked, and in some instances ignored completely.

Jewish group life at the turn of the century had none of the structural sophistication characteristic of subsequent communal endeavor. The initiators of the Conference had neither tradition nor precedent to follow in convening such an assembly. Thus, the extent of their logistical and organizational errors was so broad that, in a sense, it tended to overshadow the intrinsic purposes and achievements of the gathering.

According to *David Pinski* (1872-1959) the idea for such a conclave emerged in the course of a session held in his home, late spring 1908. We learn from an exchange of correspondence that at about this time an open meeting had been convened with the intent of creating a movement whose avowed aim would be to gain recognition for Yiddish as the national language. It was suggested that the parley be held that summer somewhere in Austria. *Dr. Alexander Harkavy* (1863-1939) outlined the goals of the conference in such a manner as to prevent Hebraists from scuttling it. He was followed by *Dr. Nathan Birnbaum* (1864-1937) convener, and then by *Dr. Chaim Zhitlovsky* (1865-1943), theoretician and prime mover of the entire undertaking.

The result was a printed invitation circular, distributed to a select list of personalities and editors of the Jewish press. It was signed by Dr. Nathan Birnbaum, Jacob Gordon, A.M. Evalenko, David Pinski and Dr. Chaim Zhitlovsky.

In response to the invitation, *Y.L. Peretz* (1852-1915) and his close friend *Jacob Dineson* (1856-1919) co-signed a letter rejecting the idea as being banal and vulgar. They maintained that it would be impossible to attract the finest Jewish litterateurs in Europe to such a symposium if the spirit and agenda as suggested were to obtain. As an alternative approach they offered the following items for consideration: (a) orthography (b) grammar (c) the Press (d) literature (e) drama (f) the importance of Yiddish as a national or folk language and its relationship to Hebrew (g) the moral obligation among peoples to preserve their literary treasures.

Despite the Presidium's acceptance in principle of this impressive list, some delegates objected to the agenda's structure and persistently raised extraneous issues. In several instances they either recalled matters which had already been resolved, or attempted to close off discussion on subjects which the majority of delegates considered significant.

Nevertheless, the Conference fulfilled an important function in that it provided a platform for some leading literary luminaries who utilized this occasion to reveal essential philosophic motivations inherent in their creativity. A few Polish publicists felt that although Yiddish literature was still comparatively young, it had been compartmentalized into three distinct schools. They contended that the American writers preferred a superficial style, full of raucous metaphors and thundering exaggerations, devoid of beauty or cadence. The Russians were partial to far-fetched fantasy and seemed to be disembodied, poetic souls, without a trace of humor. The Galicians found themselves on the horns of a dilemma, occasionally borrowing from the Americans and at other times looking to the Russians. The prospects that these diverse styles could ever be fused were slim indeed. Naively it was assumed that when the representatives of these respective schools will have met in Czernowitz they would be able to enhance and enrich their literary output through discussion and probing.

The Jewish community of Czernowitz viewed this Conference as an historic high point. For the first time they would be able to welcome some of the most prominent personalities of the Jewish literary world. Among those who indicated their intention to attend were: Samuel Eisenstadt (Berne), Sholem Asch (Koszmer), Gershon Bader (Lemberg), Buchsboim (Kolomay), Dr. Nathan Birnbaum (Czernowitz), Moshe Leib Halpern (Zlowczow), Abraham Heisler (Galicia), Beinreb (Buczaz, Galicia), Abraham Veviarke (Tchenstokhov), Michael Weichert (Galicia), Dr. Chaim Zhitlovsky (New York), Leibel Toibish (Czernowitz), Moshe Teitch (Russia), L. Chazanovich (Lemberg), Mattatyahu Miese (Przemysl), H.D. Nomberg (Warsaw), Y.L. Peretz (Warsaw), Esther Frumkin (Vilna), Lazar Kahan (Lodz), Y. Kissman (Tchernowitz), Anselm Kleinman (Lemberg), Yonah Kreppel (Cracow), Abraham Reisen (Cracow).

A fortnight before the Conference, *Morris Rosenfeld* (1862-1923), of the New York *Forward*, pointed out that with the exception of a few writers, no one in America had a serious interest in the undertaking because they failed to detect any practical value. He further indicated that the average Yiddish journalist, like his readers, attached little importance to uniform spelling or a generally accepted grammatical structure. The only essential aspect was that the reader understand what the writer produces. He grudgingly admitted that for the majority of his colleagues, including the more gifted ones, Yiddish was used as a way-station toward mastering the language of their host country, which every Jew in the Diaspora must learn if he is to survive.

Abraham Goldberg (1883-1942), writing in the *American Hebrew*, indicated that it was an open secret that the Conference was organized by two secularist Jews, Dr. Chaim Zhitlovsky and Dr. Nathan Birnbaum. Both were ardent partisans of Yiddish and shared the firm conviction that it could stave off assimilation. However, he insisted that Yiddish, which is really a *jargon*, will ultimately disappear and that only Hebrew has a bright future.

The invitation provided *Tzivion* (Dr. Benzion Hoffman, 1874-1954) with an opportunity to vent his spleen on the Yiddish press in America, which he thought was on the lowest level. Each newspaper had its category of mistakes. Every writer had a parochial conception of the language. Even the Socialist publications did not rise above this plateau of mediocrity. The dilution of classic Yiddish with English loan words, whether appropriate or otherwise, pointed to the common malady of all publications. He grudgingly conceded that there were exceptions. However, they merely proved the rule.

The underlying motivation for the Conference was articulated by Dr. Chaim Zhitlovsky when he declared that a national language is one spoken by the masses and is also the basis of its enlightenment. Neither Hebrew nor Yiddish is entitled to the appellation "national language," because the people no longer speak the former, nor is the latter the basis of cultivation and education of the intelligentsia. The task is to elevate Yiddish to the plane of the national tongue by forging it into a popularistic, cultural instrumentality.

Although the avowed purpose of the Conference was to examine the status of Yiddish, it was obvious from the outset that the component groups represented were determined to espouse their respective ideologies with regard to nationalism, socialism, cultural development, and aesthetic creativity.

In his opening statement (August 30, 1908), Dr. Nathan Birnbaum, an initiator of the Conference, challenged the allegation that Jews have too little power in the world. They needlessly ignore the limitless potentialities of a language which can provide cultural authenticity, and open wide the doors of national recognition and human rights. This represents mastery and might, particularly since Jews find themselves on the threshold of a new era. They have but to use the language lovingly, and develop it fruitfully, so that it becomes a handmaiden for cultural efflorescence and national revival.

Baal Machshoves (Dr. Isidore Eliashev, 1873-1924), who coined the phrase "bi-lingualism in a single literature," pointed out that the Czernowitz Conference, out of excessive zeal and identification with the Jewish people, overlooked the fact that literatteurs are essentially *Jewish* writers who live in an age of bi-lingualism. He also contended that the reader should not make a distinction between a Hebrew and Yiddish author. *Mendele Moicher Seforim* (1835-1917), *Chaim Nahman Bialik* (1873-1934), *Sholem Aleichem* (1859-1916), *Micha Josef Berdichewsky* (1865-1921), *Mordecai Fierberg* (1874-1899) and others were representative of the warp and woof of Jewish literary life. They were Jewish artists even though not all of them created in both languages. He further held that as long as Jews are in the unique position of being able to employ two languages in the development of one literature, it would be indefensible to give one tongue priority over the other.

He therefore suggested that the following tenets be adopted with regard to Yiddish and Hebrew: (a) wherever possible there be State recognition of Yiddish in the totality of Jewish life, to include schools, courts, and all social institutions with which Jews have contact (b) wherever feasible there be State acknowledgement of Hebrew as the national, classic language which binds Jews as a people to their glorious, historic past and nationalist aspirations. Educators and religious leaders should likewise assess the proper place of Hebrew in Jewish life and its appropriate uses.

For Baal Machshoves the question of bi-lingualism was not theoretical. He considered it an integral part of the Jewish mindset. It should be noted that *Simon Dubnow* (1860-1941) shared this opinion while going a step further. He was convinced that Jews must remain a *tri-lingual* people. Monism, or even dualism, are inadequate and would create a disability for a large segment of the Jewish population for whom Russian is the vernacular. Hence one must accept the basic tri-lingualism of European Jews. The concept of national unity in the Diaspora had to be reconciled with the multi-lingualism of a single culture for the Jewish people.

Dubnow evinced scant hope that the classical language (Hebrew) of the Jewish people would become the tongue of the Diaspora. Likewise, it would have been a grave oversight to denigrate the most potent weapon available for stemming the tide of assimilation, i.e., the folk language. However, the more amenable among the Yiddishists took a neutral course and pointed to the many writers who wrote simultaneously in both languages. They looked upon literature as an expression of the aggregate of Jewish life and would, therefore, not be drawn into a controversy over the primacy of Yiddish.

Esther Frumkin, in an impassioned address to the Conference, suggested that each social group develops its culture according to a particular outlook, as well as in the light of its political and social interests. The level of progress advocated by a chauvinist nationalist is frequently not analogous with that of a proletarian ideologist. The same cultural treasures, which are of prime importance to the proletariat, are frequently of little value to the bourgeoise, and *vice versa*.

She expanded on the contention of the *Bundists* who held that Yiddish developed because of a mass desire to live as secularists. The flowering of the language and literature was due to contiguity with other cultures, and to the need for the many, for whom Hebrew was a closed book, to express their deep feelings and aspirations. Yiddish became the medium for the intimate folksong, fantasy story, and entertainment outlets.

Several rabbis of the time sensed the danger inherent in secularism and thus resorted to every available means of combatting it. They placed a ban on the Yiddish *Sidur* (prayer book) and also forbade use of the ethical book *Simchas Hanefesh* (Joy of the Soul) which was a Yiddish translation of sections of the *Shulchon Oruch* (the authoritative compendium of Jewish religious laws). The objective was to malign Yiddish as a viable language, and thereby raise the prestige of Hebrew.

In the course of the Conference, Y.L. Peretz clarified his position concerning Yiddish. He suggested that it is not German. Jews know no German, and Germans know no Yiddish. The fact that Yiddish may at one time have been a form of German is of no consequence, so long as it did not remain as such. It became Yiddish because it is the mother tongue of ninety percent of the Jewish people, for whom it is a language and not a *jargon* or dialect. However, Yiddish was still not a *national* language. A national language evolves from, and develops along with the people. It encompasses the sum total of its cultural achievements in all places and at all times. Abraham, Isaac, Jacob, the Prophets, the later classical writers, knew no Yiddish. Just as the contemporary intelligentsia must resort to the language of their host country, so Yiddish must inevitably rely on Hebrew. Actually Jews live in a world of three tongues: the people – in Yiddish; the half assimilated intelligentsia – in the local vernacular; the Jewish intelligentsia – in the former national language of their past (Hebrew).

Which language then, he questioned, should be the Jews' national tongue subsequently? Obviously, local languages cannot fulfill such a function. Indeed they are anti-national. By adopting the language of their host country Jews would sign their death warrant by oral communication. Should the language of the future be Hebrew? It is impossible to resurrect a language artificially. One cannot believe in dead languages for living people. Therefore, there remains only Yiddish. Without the vernacular Jews would become culturally impoverished. Without Hebrew the People has no past. Without Yiddish the Jews have no People.

Thus, Peretz concluded, the folk language will of necessity become a national tongue. Jews will have to create such a plethora of cultural treasures that the knowledgeable, interested ones among them, will be able to live out their lives primarily with Yiddish. They will also have to transpose all the great religious works of the past into Yiddish, for it will have become the language of the entire People, everywhere and for all time. The trend of the cohesive, global Jewish People is inexorably towards a national language. All other living languages will become merely contiguous and strange tongues. Uniquely, Hebrew will remain the multifaceted language of the Jew's glorious heritage – his holy tongue.

It was in this spirit that he lamented the disappearance of that cadre of yeshiva students who, with their extensive rabbinic background, vanished into the broad world. They have been succeeded by a generation of ignoramuses who must, despite themselves, seek roots in the Jewish past. Gentiles took the Bible and turned it into a distinctive branch of science. Jews, on the other hand, have *ba'alay kriah* (Hebrew: Torah readers) in their synagogues who read the Bible out loud by rote, and are followed in like fashion by the congregants. This merely highlights the need to be thoroughly familiar with the text and significance of Scriptures, because each culture must have its own traditions, historic continuum, and distinctive values.

Sholem Asch (1880-1957) indicated that the question whether or not Yiddish is a national language is identical with the dilemma concerning Jewish nationhood. Yiddish has the same right to be designated as the national tongue as do Jews a nation. Yiddish is no strange offspring to them. It is the fruit of their blood and heart. Whoever is sensitive to Yiddish knows that it is their national tongue. With regard to Hebrew, Asch would have considered it a second *Tisha B'av* (destruction of the Temple in ancient Jerusalem) if it were to pass into oblivion. However, he maintained, there are two Hebrew languages, that of the *Patriarchs*, *Prophets* and *Midrashim* – the living, natural Hebrew, beloved and respected by Yiddishists more than by Hebraists – and the new Hebrew spoken in Palestine. The latter is synthetic and unnatural, hence, not authentic Hebrew.

Secularists took the firm position that a language spoken by eight to nine million people is unquestionably to be considered *a* language. The only reservation might be that Yiddish is not recognized as *the* national tongue of the Jewish people. However, they stoutly rejected the contention that Yiddish is merely a *jargon* which includes German, Hebrew and Slavic words. It is as distinctive as any other vernacular because all of them contain a substantial number of loan words. They included modern Hebrew in this rubric, and went a step further by insisting that it has lost its very soul and must be viewed in the same light as ancient Greek or Latin. Hebrew should be considered as a link with the past and as an instrumentality for bridging time.

Ahad Ha'am (Asher Ginsburg, 1856-1927) characterized the Conference as a convention of boors gathered for the purpose of denigrating Hebrew. He expressed the hope that in the course of its efflorescence it should never be confronted by a more threatening opponent than that pathetic *jargon* which one day appears in Czernowitz at a conference, and soon thereafter finds itself entombed.

Shortly after the turn of the 20th century there emerged a synthesis of Zionist and Socialist thought. Groups were formed spontaneously in all parts of Russia, Vilna, Warsaw, Odessa, Minsk, Crimea, Ekaterinoslav, Rostov. The distinguishing features of the respective aggregations were their motivation and orientation. The common denominator was the attempt to reconcile Zionism with Socialism. Thus they were differentiated from the assimilated proletarian movement on the one hand, and from the general, nationalistic camp, devoid of socialistic tendencies and class interests, on the other. Most of these cells were soon to be identified under the collective name of *Poale Zion* (Workers of Zion), and aligned themselves on the following issues: the political struggle in their host country; the question of a national language: Hebrew or Yiddish; whether to be pro-Palestine or territorialistic.

The most vigorous source of opposition to Labor Zionism appeared at the opposite end of the ideological spectrum in the form of the *Algemayner Yidisher Arbeter Bund in Russland un Poilen* (General Jewish Labor Association in Russia and Poland), founded in September 1897, by representatives of several Russian Jewish political parties, gathered in Vilna for that purpose. Thus was opened a new chapter in the history of the Jewish class struggle, its search for emancipation and new social forms. They strongly advocated a joint campaign with laborers and Socialists of other ethnic groups. However, inasmuch as non-Jewish workers, by and large, lacked the cultural and political sophistication of their Jewish compatriots, the *Bund* undertook to organize them in order to facilitate a common economic and political program for the entire Russian proletariat.

Some activists in the *Bund* strongly advocated integrating Jews into the general Russian working class. Among those who expressed this opinion vociferously were *Leon Trotsky* (1879-1940), *Pavel Axelrod* (1850-1928), and *Julius Martov* (1873-1923). They objected to the "autonomous" stand of the *Bund*, and its posturing as the sole representative of a separatist Jewish proletariat. Reluctantly they considered allowing them to deliberate in Yiddish on the assumption that many of its members knew neither Polish nor Russian. However, under no circumstances were they prepared to accept the Bundist conception of nationhood as applied to Jews in the Diaspora.

At this juncture the *Bund* was compelled to crystallize its nationalistic approach, not only in relation to its striving against assimilationists in the Russian Social-Democratic party, but also with regard to Zionism and other nationalist concepts percolating in the Jewish masses. The urgency stemmed from a wide psychological and ideological chasm which existed between the two. The *Bund* was the first Jewish political party organized primarily for the purpose of conducting a common struggle for equality among all people. Thus, while propagandizing in a systematic manner, they insisted that Jews abandon their obsequiousness, because they are entitled to the same egalitarian status as the population at large.

It should be noted that the relatively sparse amount of source material and memoirs available from the various communities of the early founders stands in sharp contrast to Vilna, the cradle of the *Bund*. Minsk, for example, had similar propaganda cells which, in fact, began operation in 1883, three years before Vilna. The human material was essentially the same, yet the impact on the movement as a whole was scarcely perceptible. Although there were some dynamic personalities, the concept did not touch an appreciable number of adherents.

Vilna was the logical locale for such an organization because it was the most dynamic Jewish center in Eastern Europe. It was the locus of the Polanized, Lithuanian, progressive intelligentsia, as well as of the

Russified Poles. As for Jews, despite the harsh times endured in the last quarter of the 19th century, they enjoyed a rich spiritual life which expressed itself in a multifaceted cultural atmosphere on a variety of levels.

Pioneers of the *Bund* maintained that because of its unique characteristics, only Vilna could have produced a Jewish labor movement with international ramifications, yet devoid of the inferiority complex manifested by some of the Jewish intelligentsia in other cities. They pointed to Warsaw where, for example, attempts were made to adopt the Polish life-style while rejecting basic Jewishness, even to the extent of scoffing at Yiddish as a "jargon."

At the outset, several leading proponents considered their work in Vilna as temporary, a sort of preparation for the forthcoming revolutionary spadework to be done among the Russian masses, when they will have succeeded in breaching the barriers of parochial Jewish activism into the non-Jewish world. This approach was hardly in consonance with reality. Since the late 1880s Jewish workers had already demonstrated that they were not passive people. True, they had not yet mounted a genuine class struggle, but they had engaged in a concerted attempt to free themselves from the stifling conditions of their mundane, depressing situation. Interestingly enough, many women workers were in the vanguard of these efforts.

Although Vilna was regarded as a dynamic cultural center, it nevertheless had a palpably provincial quality about it. There was a wide gulf between the dreams of the parochial intelligentsia and the grim actualities of the outside world. The Bundists' perceptions of the scope and potential of the Social Democratic party were severely limited. They were indecisive about methods of propagating Marxist theory within society in general, and the labor group in particular. They had no notion of organizational techniques in relation to high-density populations, particularly in extremely concentrated industrial centers.

By the early 1890s, the Vilna group had laid the basis for a mass movement. Concurrently, the distinctively Jewish dimension manifested itself, and ultimately surfaced as *"Bundism."* The idea of a general Russian conference with a special Jewish section probably emerged at this time, on the assumption that it would be more feasible to convene like-minded unions rather than fragmented cells. Whatever the case, it was the determination of the leaders that the Jewish fractions should join the general Russian party as a unit.

Bundists proceeded on the premise that Jewish life in the Diaspora can, and must, be a productive experience, while allowing the Jew to retain his identity as he integrates fully into the host society. Hence they differed sharply with Zionists who maintained that the Jew can achieve equal status only in terms of a viable Jewish state in Palestine. Theoretically, the Bundists might have evolved a synthesis between these two positions. However, the revolutionary climate of that time precluded such a possibility. They regarded Zionism as utopian and concluded that it could achieve its goals only through diplomatic negotiation with the bourgeoisie – something which was anathema to them.

The two movements also came into conflict on the cultural level. Bundism made a signal contribution to the development of a secularist Jewish perspective, as well as to the renaissance of the Yiddish language, literature, and press. Zionism, on the other hand, continued in the pattern of the *Haskalah* and insisted that the language of the Bible cannot be separated from the people of the Bible nor the land of the Bible.

In its persistent struggle with Zionism, the *Bund* was compelled to sharp-focus its definition of Jewish nationhood. Although it peremptorily rejected assimilationist tendencies of the Jewish intelligentsia, it was just as violently opposed to the Zionist conception of the Jewish People as a universal nation. The cultural autonomists among the Bundists maintained that an historic background alone does not qualify a people to think of itself as a nation. It must also have a vibrant language and literature, with a cultural common denominator. The Jews could be considered a people only insofar as it is united in its striving for national recognition and cultural autonomy.

Pragmatically, they organized a series of social groups, dramatic circles and choirs, which functioned as camouflage for many illegal political activities, and also provided opportunities to intensify their cultural identification with the Jewish People. Although founders of the *Bund* were, in the main, products of the Hebraistic *Haskalah*, nevertheless, they sensed that Jewish masses could be reached only through the vernacular. Consequently, Socialist literature for the proletariat was produced in rather simple Yiddish, even though some of the more prominent Jewish writers of the time employed belletristic forms in stating their revolutionary ideologies. These illegal brochures, printed abroad as well as in Russia, were distributed in thousands of copies.

A series of resolutions were presented toward the final session of the Conference: *Y.L. Peretz*: The Conference recognizes Yiddish as a language of the Jewish People and urges the unification of Jewish culture with the Yiddish language. (*Yonah Kreppel* offered the following amendment: The preceding resolution is not intended to diminish the signficance and value of Hebrew for the Jewish People.) *Esther Frumkin:* The Conference recognizes Yiddish as the only national language of the Jewish People. Hebrew has the status of an historic monument whose revival would constitute an Utopia. *L. Khazanovich*: Yiddish is a national language of the Jewish People, and in those countries where compact masses of Jews reside, we demand full political, social and civil rights. *Chaim Zhitlovsky, Sholem Asch, H.D. Nomberg*: Yiddish is the national language of the Jewish People. However, each delegate to the Conference, and members of the projected organization, is at liberty to view Hebrew according to the dictates of his personal convictions.

The Conference ended with the ambiguous conclusion that Yiddish is to be considered *a* – not *the* – national language of the Jewish People. Obviously, such a compromise could satisfy neither camp. Nevertheless, the Yiddishists claimed a victory, because for the first time the primacy of the folk tongue had found an important niche in the deliberations of an international Jewish conclave.

The final item on the agenda was the proposal that a telegram be sent to *Mendele Moicher Seforim* expressing the appreciation of those present at the Conference. *Buchboim* suggested that a similar message be sent to *Sholem Aleichem*. His motion was defeated on the grounds that comparable greetings would have to go to all famous Jewish writers, whereas it was generally accepted that *Mendele* was the "*Zayde*" (grandfather) – in fact, the symbol of Yiddish literature.

After the close of business, Dr. Nathan Birnbaum, newly elected President of the Central Committee, summarized the achievements of the Conference and outlined its projections. He indicated that much of value had been accomplished, including demonstrations, which in themselves have a modicum of importance. He further pointed out that the Conference embraced a plethora of opinions and trends in Jewish life. Polemicizing concerning Yiddish had unique meaning, inasmuch as this was the first time such discussion took place in an open forum, thus providing many of the participants with insights which will enable them to deal with the question more intelligently in the future. Representatives of the respective movements and points of view who participated in the Conference did so out of love for their People and its culture.

Regretfully, as so often happens in Jewish life, in lieu of creating an atmosphere of mutual respect and understanding, the Conference led to a period of base recriminations and irrational caviling on the part of extremists from the several camps. Yiddishists enjoyed "burying" Hebrew with the same enthusiasm that Hebraists prophesied the imminent demise of Yiddish. Rather than enhancing Jewish culture, each group in its distinctive manner, instead of joining forces to protect itself from external and internal dangers, systematically proceeded to destroy the other. The language issue took on the character of a cultural battle, as well as an inter-party struggle. Every meeting, whether social or intellectual, somehow turned into an explosive confrontation between Hebraists and Yiddishists.

In all likelihood this gross conduct stemmed from the bitter disappointment sensed by Socialist oriented intelligentsia following the disastrous first Russian revolution (1905). Included were loyal Bundists and Socialist Zionists who had become entrenched in the various culture groups and literary or dramatic circles. This applied particularly to the Zionist Youth movement which devoted more of its attention to cultural matters than political activity. Hence the almost frenzied manner in which they threw themselves into this fray.

Actually, this was not the sole reason for the conflict. Objectively, it should be noted that Yiddish had become a palpable competitor of Hebrew. New forces appeared in the Jewish communal arena. The working masses, mostly uneducated and led by Jewish revolutionaries, all spoke and read Yiddish, whereas the recognized intelligentsia favored Russian which, they hoped, would become the medium enabling them to "elevate" their brethren to the level of general revolutionary activism. This might have been possible had they confined their disseminatory efforts to small cells. However, as the Socialist leadership moved from propaganda to agitation, and expanded its sphere of activity, they had to resort to Yiddish, even if it meant confronting the need to learn the language themselves.

While attempting to reach the majority of their brethren they had no alternative but to broaden their language skills. Furthermore, in the course of arguing in behalf of equality and status for the Jewish working class they also had to stress the importance of its folk tongue, particularly in view of the campaign for civil rights which quickly evolved into a battle for national recognition and Jewish cultural autonomy, with Yiddish as its spoken tongue. This followed quite logically, inasmuch as Yiddish was the preferred language of this period, with an ever increasing degree of acceptability, not only ideologically but also practically. It was reflected in the burgeoning press, literature and theater. There emerged a symbiotic relationship between Yiddish culture and the masses as a result of heightened awareness and activism. Thus was formed the instrument of expression for their spiritual enhancement and communal efforts.

But Socialists were not the only ones to participate in this renaissance of the Yiddish language. Concurrently, as that movement filled the average Jewish worker with pride, stimulated his motivation, and deepened his desire for knowledge in general, so nationalism, and particularly Zionism, aroused the national consciousness of the Jewish folk masses. Just as the Socialists used Yiddish to create an attractive political climate, so did the Zionists to further their ideological purposes by means of a series of periodicals, including *Der Yud* (The Jew) and *Dos Yidische Folk* (The Jewish People). The foregoing, plus the accumulated inner strengths of the Jewish community, resulted not only in an expanded Labor press and literature, but also in a fully developed Yiddish world of letters. And so dawned a new epoch in the history of the Yiddish word.

Regretfully, the Yiddishists became more assertive, overbearing, and aggressive, while some of the Hebraists tended to panic in face of this rising cultural tide. The jealous ones among them viewed Yiddishism as a new ideology, as an objective force, or simply as a language which is rapidly evolving into the dominant component of modern, Jewish cultural life. Thus, both the subjective and objective factors inherent in the clash between Hebraism and Yiddishism brought the adherents of each language to an irreversible parting of the ways.

Chapter VIII

Niger, like many of his contemporaries, was deeply distressed by the discord between the respective proponents of the two languages, which manifested itself before 1914 and increased in intensity after World War I. As a result of wartime upheavals, dislocations, and pogroms, hundreds of thousands of Jews were uprooted from their homes where they had lived for generations. Many of these hapless people were drained spiritually as well as physically. Children were the prime sufferers, since they were deprived of all elementary educational opportunities, either religious or secular, to say nothing about the possibility of secondary school or university attendance. Consequently, this considerable portion of the Jewish community was in no condition to become part of a cultural continuum predicated on the concept of bi-lingualism. Most of them had difficulty coping with one language and its literary forms. The meager shreds of culture they may have retained evaporated in the course of their wanderings.

The post-war period was characterized by the largest wave of migration in all Jewish history. The need for resettlement was so great during the War years that Jews hazarded everything in order to escape the European gehenna. No sooner was the war over than Jewish emigration spiralled upward – in 1921, close to 120,000 came into the United States alone. Add the immigration into Palestine and South America, and the figure for the first normal year after the War exceeded 150,000. Had it not been for quotas that were soon enacted, Jewish immigration in the post-war era would have been ever increasingly higher.

Any cultural propensities these people may have had before the War disappeared in the trauma of what for many was aimless wandering. When the more fortunate succeeded in landing at some beckoning port they were confronted by the gargantuan task of adjusting to the geographic, political, and economic conditions of their new environment. Culturally – except for the unusual few – they took the path of least resistance. From a socio-psychological point of view, particularly with regard to Jewish education, literature, and social contacts, that meant mono-lingualism.

Two new, yet radically different Jewish population centers arose after the War. Each was determined to make it virtually impossible for Jews to pursue their cultural life in the traditional bi-lingual mode. First was Palestine – the "Jewish Homeland" – which, under the impact of the Balfour Declaration (1917) began to take on the outlines of a State. The other was the compact Jewish community of the emerging Soviet Union.

In both cases leaders had distinctive objectives and specific guidelines for achieving them. The Palestinian venue was national/revolutionary, the means – social control, whereas the Soviet Union's social/revolutionary goals could be reached only via a dictatorship of the proletariat. The common denominator between these two disparate approaches was their conscious and organized opposition to the Jewish tradition of bi-lingualism. Every attempt was made in the evolving *Yishuv* (Jewish settlement in Palestine) to minimize – or even eliminate – the influence of Yiddish as an educational and cultural factor. The Soviet Union's draconian measures were so extensive that only faint memories of a vibrant Jewish culture remained.

The Jewish section of the Communist Party (*Yevsectzia*) was intent upon achieving "national cultural autonomy." Thus, with the perseverance of party hacks, they tried to outdo their Russian colleagues in the race to rid themselves of "old world tendencies" (read: the entire historical heritage of the Jewish people). Such was their appointed task, and they succeeded fully. They demeaned Jewish religion in keeping with the general principle of atheism; synagogues were turned into workers' clubs; *hedorim* (elementary religious classes) and *yeshives* (houses of rabbinic studies) were forbidden to function openly; it was illegal to print and disseminate all forms of Hebrew literature. Language autonomy was restricted to the "true" Yiddish, with its new orthography that eliminated any vestige of relationship with Hebrew.

All Zionist groups, including the Socialist ones, were persistently harassed because of their tie to "British imperialism." Many members were imprisoned or even sent to Siberia. There was nothing Jewish about their schools except for the language of instruction. Children were indoctrinated with a sense of class hatred which included their "bourgeoisie" parents, as well as a rejection of Jewish nationalist values. In State schools the Government established "attack cadres" of *Komsomol* (Communist Youth Organization) for the purpose of carrying out the Communist world revolution.

Under such oppressive circumstances one could hardly envision a period of freely expressed Jewish learning and literature. The universities of Moscow, Kiev, and Minsk established Yiddish sections which published "academic" works saturated with narrow, party sloganeering. The Yiddish press, like its general counterpart, was a government monopoly. Regional sections of the *Yevsectzia* published three Yiddish newspapers: *Emes* (Truth) in Moscow, *Shtern* (Star) in Kharkov, *Oktyaber* (October) in Minsk. Their avowed purpose was blatant propaganda. The creative dimension was dependent on "Socialist invitations" – stories, poems, commentaries – written and edited according to authorized guidelines. Ignorance and incompetence were the order of the day. Any manifestation of talent was immediately suppressed.

Here the similarity between the two newly emerging Jewish population centers ends. For Palestine, in keeping with the classic definition of Zionism – the aspiration toward bringing together the People of the Bible, in the land of the Bible, with the language of the Bible – the integration of Hebrew into their daily lives became an almost natural process, albeit consciously (and in some instances obsessively) effected. Yiddish was scorned by the majority, and in many cases rejected outright by educators, writers, opinion makers and politicians, on the grounds that its use was a throwback to the disastrous Diaspora from which they fled. The preference for and use of Hebrew as the vernacular of the people was a strictly cultural decision that was implemented fairly painlessly and practically without rancor.

Hence, in addition to the social/psychological schism between Hebrew and Yiddish, there accrued the more practical geographical/political dimension. Palestine became the center for Hebrew exclusively, whereas Soviet Russia, having boycotted Hebrew, made Yiddish the official language of Jewish culture. Inevitably, this changed the concept of "two tongues – one literature" into a pair of distinctive literatures, each in a different language. This was not merely an example of clashing ideologies but rather a manifestation of political/geographic entrenchment on the part of a mono-lingual society. Thus Soviet-Jewish literature became devoid of any traditional Hebraic concepts. On the other hand, it should be noted, that the Hebrew literary output of Palestine had ceased drawing from the well of Yiddish life, while its educational system had all but eliminated Yiddish values from its educational system. In Palestine this could only have resulted in a generation of litterateurs totally ignorant of Yiddish, whereas in the Soviet Union it will have produced a group of writers incapable of appreciating the intimate dependence of Yiddish on authentic Hebrew sources.

Niger was disturbed by the fact that partiality toward mono-lingualism prevalent in both Palestine and the Soviet Union had begun to take root in other lands of Jewish settlement. In the decades of the 1920s and 30s the problem was no longer that of Hebrew *and* Yiddish but rather the alternative of Hebrew *or* Yiddish. With keen prescience he foresaw the disappearance of that passionate partisanship toward bi-lingualism which had characterized previous generations.

The danger manifested itself in the tendency of younger literary historians to ignore the relationship earlier Hebrew writers had with Yiddish, as well as the bond Yiddish literature had with its Hebraic heritage. They treated the history of Yiddish literature as if it had a separate existence by overlooking the fact that, on the one hand, old Yiddish literature in bygone days was, in effect, "the women's section of the synagogue" (their religious tie), and, on the other, the homely meeting place for the "common man." Also, they generally ignored the reality that these people for whom Yiddish literature was originally created, viewed it as a sort of cultural pathfinder.

During this transition period a concerted effort was made by some lexicographers and philologists to raise Yiddish to the level of other European languages. In the process of word crafting, rather than relying on the Hebrew/Aramaic sources inherent in Yiddish, they preferred the German/Romance aspects. Obviously, the secularistic nature of this approach blended easily with the intent of these younger literary historians to secularize Jewish culture generally. They looked to external, worldly works – as opposed to the Jewish religious, or half-religious literature – which grew on homely soil, and sank deep roots. They tried to create the illusion that the less a Yiddish piece reflects the Jewish life-style and its cultural heritage, and the less original it is, so much the greater will be its impact.

The eminent literary historian, *Dr. Israel Zinberg* (1873-1939), maintained that Yiddish literature is the embodiment of Jewish cultural life and is intimately bound with its Hebrew/Aramaic heritage. While neither denying nor denigrating the importance of contiguous literatures, he stressed the centrality of the bi-lingual tradition and its influence on the folk tongue, as well as on the Jewish cultural epoch. As a pre-World War I figure, he was a dominant voice among those writers who stoutly defended the validity of bi-lingualism, as opposed to that group of Yiddishist literary historians who, during the 1920s and 30s, contended that Yiddish should go it alone. Contrariwise, the circle of Hebraist literary historiographers, led by *Dr. Joseph Klausner* (1874-1958) of Jerusalem, strived to minimize the role of Yiddish, if not to eliminate it altogether.

The spirit of cultural isolationism encountered hardly any resistance during these two decades. True, there were some educational institutions which tried to stand by the principle of bi-lingualism, like the *Folkshulen* (Folk schools) and the *Lehrer Seminar* (Teachers Seminary) of the *Yidish Natzionaln Arbeter Farband in Amerika* (Jewish National Workers Alliance of America), as well as the religious *Bnos Yaakov Shulen in Poilen* (Daughters of Jacob Schools of Poland). In this vein, there was a limited number of European and American writers whose by-lines were to be found in both literatures.

Nevertheless, the general tendency was one of separateness, particularly on the part of Yiddish writers. Hebrew litterateurs, from their side, could not forget Yiddish even had they so desired because, with few exceptions, they were all raised in a Yiddish-speaking atmosphere. Ironically, the Yiddishists, who had no Hebraic grounding whatsoever, found their numbers increasing markedly after World War I, primarily in America and the Soviet Union. They could not make Hebrew their literary medium simply because they did not know the language; had never studied Bible or Talmud; had no familiarity with modern Hebrew literature. Hebrew writers, on the other hand, including those who lived in Palestine, knew Yiddish, despite the fact they had no use for it.

Withal that, this period saw numerous translations of classic Hebrew works – ranging from aggadic selections; extracts of writings by *Rashi* (1040-1105), *Maimonides* (1135-1204), and leading poets of the Golden Age of Spain – to modern historians, poets, novelists, and dramatists.

Unwaveringly, Niger remained fast to the conviction that *Hasidism*, *Enlightenment*, *Zionism*, *Folkism*, the struggle for human and national rights, these many manifestations of renaissance and aspiration, could only lead to a multi-faceted development of the people's language, art and literature. It was pre-ordained. Yiddishism was the expression of historical ineluctability.

This same dimension of historic inevitability also motivated the renewal process of Hebrew and its literature. The identical forces and movements that lent vitality to Yiddishism did the same for Hebraism. Obviously, none of the dominant trends in Jewish life in those times could have been effective with either Yiddish or Hebrew alone. Both languages proved useful in the creative strivings of thinkers and writers. This led to the conclusion that those who looked upon Jewish history and development as a cultural whole must accept the principle of bi-lingualism.

However, in reality this proved to be an illusion. Historically oriented intellectuals could not abide those who, pursuant to Mendele's metaphor, would prefer to breathe through one nostril at a time. The logical determination was, therefore, that the Jewish literary world had been split because of the turmoil that obtained in Jewish life, resulting from partisanship and strict party loyalty that spilled over into its cultural life.

* * *

The rise of Nazism, the outbreak of World War II and the Holocaust that ensued convinced Niger that history has a frightening streak of ruthlessness. Thus it was with great difficulty that he accepted the grim reality of the surviving, decimated Jewish people standing on the threshold of a vastly different era of cultural aspiration. The destruction of Eastern European Jewry brought down the curtain on that glorious epoch of Yiddishist literary and cultural creativity which peaked during the 1920s and 30s. The death knell was sounded for the "Hebrew and/or Yiddish" controversy. Henceforth, the "third language" (which Dubnow advocated from the turn of the century on) became the vernacular of all Jewish communities throughout the world, except for Palestine, and after 1948, Israel.

As late as 1954 (about a year before his death) he stubbornly maintained that despite the rapid disappearance of Yiddish as the central language factor among Diaspora Jews, every possible effort should be made to bolster its former status and influence. For him the crucial issue was retention of Jewish identity. He suggested, that as long as Jews hold on to Yiddish, how ever more they hew to their values while increasing the spiritual/nationalistic treasures which stem from that background, so much greater will be the human resources at their side, as they start on the road toward integration into the new environment and larger society.

Nevertheless, he reluctantly admitted that it would indeed be quixotic to attempt such an infusion into the attenuated Jewish organism because the whole matter of language had become a qualitative rather than a quantitative issue. Statistics are hardly a reliable measure of contemporary life. If Jews were prone to be frightened by "tragic numbers" they, together with Yiddish, would long ago have disappeared from the face of the earth. But peoples, like languages, are not very "scientific." Specifically the Jewish people, as a folk, has a tendency to ignore prognostications based on alleged objective investigation. It has its "own" rules and refuses to be measured by the usual criteria. No statistician or sociologist could have predicted on the eve of World War II that in the course of a few accursed years hundreds of Jewish communities and millions of their inhabitants would be annihilated. By the same token it could not have been anticipated before the outbreak of World War I that shortly thereafter there would be an efflorescence of Yiddish, even amongst those who were not particularly disposed to it, that manifested itself in the form of an offical language in one country (Poland), as well as the recognized language of instruction in Jewish schools, Jewish teachers seminaries, and scientific institutes in other lands (Lithuania, Latvia, Estonia). Given the severely limited body of facts at the time, it also would have been impossible to prophesy that Hebrew would become the vernacular of the emerging and prospering State of Israel. When one is concerned with problems of language, culture, and national renaissance, rather than probing so-called reality and the realm of Jewish identity, it is more important to sow the seeds of future growth than to gaze at what has sprouted in the past.

True, it is often difficult to distinguish between means and ends. But when dealing with a perspective of the future the Jew has to bear in mind that his language, or both of them, plus his consciousness and aspirations, are not disparate entities. There is always mutual interaction.

Hebrew could not have attained its centrality in Israel had it merely relied on the normal course of events characteristic of a gradually evolving society. Were it not for a select number of individuals and groups, ideologically motivated and dedicated to this goal, such a phenomenal reality could not have come about within the short span of half a century. This has had an enormous influence on how Diaspora Jewry relates to practical needs, its sense of peoplehood and cultural identification, as well as to the State of Israel.

Niger then pondered the crucial question. Are there realistic needs and an idealistic basis that would justify the hopeless nurturing of Yiddish and Yiddishist culture as a creative force in American Jewish cultural life? Or should this dynamic, expanding community accept the verdict of history and live out its life with English, while aware of the ever expanding role of Hebrew because of the State of Israel, as Yiddish and its achievements painlessly fade into oblivion? Sadly, this applies to the entire Diaspora.

Chapter IX

Niger's dedicated concentration on the concept of bi-lingualism paralleled his almost total involvement in the issue of secularism/traditionalism. In fact, he epitomized the Yiddish translation of the term "secular": *veltlich* (worldly.) Having been steeped in rabbinic learning up to the threshold of adulthood, he proudly carried that baggage with him throughout his prolific, creative career. He spent the first half of his life in Eastern Europe as it was reeling from the upheavals of World War I and the Russian Revolution, then came to the United States, where he exerted considerable intellectual influence on the burgeoning immigrant Jewish community which was in the throes of a search for identity. Since he straddled the two major centers of Jewish settlement he could assess the achievements of the former and the needs of the latter.

During the 1920s and 30s a crucial question among the intelligentsia was the relationship of the Jew to his past. Under the impact of the Enlightenment, not only Jews, but also *Yidishkeit* (Jewishness) started breaking out of the ghetto some hundred years before. This constituted one of the most momentous turning points in Jewish history. Suddenly the Jew was confronted by a vast, unfamiliar, bewildering world. Contact and conflict with host societies created a realization of different values. Many of the psychological props Jews had resorted to suddenly disappeared: "a light unto the nations"; chosenness; superior literacy; "*a yidishe kop*" (a Jewish head). Human interaction took on a completely different cast, as did man in his relation to God. Concepts of peoplehood, nationalism, universalism and religion, which had formed the matrix of the Jewish two-millennial tradition, underwent drastic changes and, in some cases, assumed entirely new forms. Now the Jew had to find a place in society with often incomprehensible ground rules, ruthlessly imposed by the overwhelming majority on to this inconsequential minority.

Inevitably, amazing advances in the arts, sciences, and technology had an irresistible appeal for Jewish intellectuals. The age of religion abdicated in favor of the age of rationalism. Consequently, extensive secularization of major European and American cultural centers provided ample opportunity for Jews to participate in the flourishing, creative life around them.

It was relatively easy to find an harmonious accommodation between Judaism and human reason. However, the situation became more complicated when it touched on the question of moral values. Rabbinic Judaism never made a distinction between religion and secularism (only between the holy and the profane), as did Christianity. It had neither a clergy, nor a structured church, nor a social caste of religious funtionaries. According to the *Midrash* (commentary on Biblical texts) Torah was given in the wilderness to show that it was for all people equally, to the end of time. Rabbinic literature, throughout the centuries, has stressed that Judaism is a this-worldly civilization of law and order. Each individual bears personal responsibility for his actions, both in relation to his conscience as well as to society. There is no intermediary between a Jew and God, as there is no Biblical mention or assurance of salvation, nor a life after death. Judaism eschewed asceticism because it was understood to be a form of escapism. By the same token it never worshipped Nature, nor engaged in any pagan practices which stemmed from it. For the Jew enclosed in his involuted ghetto or *shtetl* (village) – Man, the universe of Torah and religious observance were far more important than the splendor of the world around him. It was inconceivable that he would interrupt his studies of rabbinic texts, look out, lift up his eyes and sigh "how beautiful is that lovely tree."

Throughout the ages Jews have been an urban people. This was a determining factor in the evolution of occupational patterns. It might also account for their distance from Nature, and the propensity for intellectual pursuits. For the Jew, Nature was often cruel, merciless, unjust and capricious. So did he view the societies around him. However, in his cocoon of Torah, he considered himself "redeemed from exile," because he felt protected in the house of study and the Jewish quarter. On the other hand, he was in constant fear the moment he set foot outside his sheltered enclave. Field and forest were a strange, hostile experience.

The rise of Hasidism affected an interesting change in the Jew's attitude towards Nature. The founder of the movement, *Rabbi Israel Ba'al Shem Tov* (1698-1760), taught that "the whole earth is filled with His Glory" (Psalms 72:14), implying that there are sparks of divinity in the natural environment. He enjoined his disciples and followers to worship the Lord in joyfulness, whenever and wherever the mood moved them. But this in no way detracted from the need for scrupulous observance of religious rules and practices.

The Enlightenment was conducive to a radical revision of generally accepted Jewish values. Hasidism may have brought the Jew closer to Nature – but it was the Enlightenment that made him aware of the culture around him, and led to a meaningful reevaluation of standards. Some *Maskilim* (Hebrew: enlighteners) went so far as to criticize severely the Jewish mores, customs, occupations and, indeed, the very essence of Jewish separateness. Undoubtedly this critique was, in a large measure, justified. However, it should be noted that in many instances it resulted from self-disparagement in face of the richness and grandeur of encompassing cultures. It was not uncommon to express unbounded admiration for everything non-Jewish, and to accept without reservation the negative assessments and opinions of Jews and Judaism on the part of Gentiles.

The denigration of the Jewish past, as well as the indigenous life-style, was not confined to assimilationists. Prevalent nationalistic movements were, essentially, a protest against the reality of the Diaspora. The call for a sovereign homeland embraced the idea that the Jewish people must be a folk like all others. There must be an end to the isolation and insecurity of the *golus* (exile).

Hence remained the question of how best to reach the Jewish masses. Intellectuals searched for an escape hatch from the quandary of bilingualism. Hebraists sought to convert "the language of the book" into "the tongue of the street," whereas Yiddishists attempted to transmute the vernacular into an instrument of modern cultural renaissance. Both efforts produced extraordinary results.

Just as inter-War Poland became the center of autonomous Jewish politics in the Diaspora, it also served as the locus of separatist Jewish culture, whether secular or religious, Hebraist or Yiddishist. The yeshives (schools of rabbinic study) for which Poland had been so famous, continued to flourish, while additional institutions of in-depth rabbinic learning were founded by two new religious parties, *Agudes Yisroel* (Association of Israel) and *Mizrachi* (Eastern). Along with the preservation of traditional Jewish culture went a remarkable experiment aimed at creating in Poland a secular Jewish national culture based on Yiddish, and designed to serve as one of the cornerstones of Jewish national autonomy. Never before in modern Jewish history, and for that matter never again, would this version of Jewish culture make such deep inroads into Jewish life. If in the Soviet Union the regime clamped down on Yiddish culture in the 1930s, and if in America acculturation and assimilation sentenced Yiddish to a gradual but inevitable decline, Poland remained the ideal setting in which the "folk language" and "folk culture" in its recent, contemporaneous form could thrive. Moreover, the unification of Congress Poland with Galicia and the eastern borderlands, while causing serious problems for Jewish politics, was a blessing in disguise for its culture. Indeed, the role of *Litvaks* (Lithuanians) in Yiddish cultural life in the capital was so great as to cause grumbling in some circles with regard to the "foreign invasion" from Lithuanian-Belorussian lands.

One dramatic example of the success of Yiddish culture in Poland was the Yiddish press, with its two mass-circulation dailies in Warsaw – *Haynt* (Today) and *Moment* (Moment), and hundreds of other daily and weekly newspapers in the provinces. Another instance was the flourishing Yiddish theater. Inter-War Poland also became a great center of Yiddish literature. True, the most celebrated native writer, *Y.L. Peretz*, died in Warsaw in 1915, and *Sholem Asch*, also of Polish birth, wrote his most famous works in America. But there likewise appeared such talented authors as *Y.Y. Trunk* (1887-1961), *Oizer Varshavsky* (1898-1944), and *I.J. Singer* (1893-1944). This was the period in which the Nobel Laureate, *Isaac Bashevis Singer* (1904-1992), known simply as *Bashevis* in Yiddish, made his literary debut. Along with literature, went the development of Yiddish literary criticism and new efforts to promote an understanding of Jewish civilization.

In 1925 *YIVO: The Jewish Scientific Institute* was founded in Vilna, mostly by secular Yiddishist intellectuals sympathetic to the *Folkists* or to Jewish Socialism. *YIVO* quickly became the main scholarly institution of the secularist Yiddish cultural movement, and its various publications helped lay the foundation for modern academic work on Yiddish language and literature. Likewise a distinguished cadre, mostly from Galicia, engaged in research under their aegis on East European Jewish history. Outstanding among them were *Majer Balaban* (1877-1942) and *Ignacy Schipper* (1884-1943), both of whom made lasting contributions to this field.

For those Jewish intellectuals committed to the cause of secular Yiddish culture, education was surely the single most important issue. It was not surprising, therefore, that tremendous efforts were made to educate the young generation in this spirit. In 1921 a conference in Warsaw created the *Central Jewish School Organization* (also known as *Tsisho* from the Yiddish acronym,) which aimed at establishing elementary and high schools that would use Yiddish as the language of instruction and promote a national, Diaspora-centered, secular Jewish culture. From the very beginning the system was highly politicized and riddled by conflicts among Bundists, Zionist-Socialists, Folkists, and even Communists. Many leaders debated endlessly such questions as whether or not the goal was to produce "class-conscious Socialists." A similar quandary related to the teaching of Hebrew. Tsisho's greatest dilemma, however, was the nature of the new secular culture it sought to promote in the classroom, for such a concept would have inevitably rejected not only Jewish religion, but Hebrew culture as well, and would have replaced them with the still very young Yiddish secular culture of Eastern Europe. There were no models in the Jewish historical experience for the kind of schools they intended to establish, and its revolutionary character, both in the sense of its Socialist ideology and radical departure from traditional Jewish education, undoubtedly alienated many parents. The success of Tsisho was also hampered by other problems which it shared with most other Jewish school networks, government harassment and the state's refusal to share the financial burden.

Granted the existence in inter-War Poland of a Yiddish literary "renaissance," how deep then, were its roots? It should be noted that despite an unparalleled flourishing of the Yiddish press, theater, and literature, the secularist Yiddish movement encountered grave difficulties, both in light of its militant secularism and because, in the final analysis, many Jews must have questioned the value of a Yiddish education for their children. It was all very well to study the works of Sholem Aleichem and Peretz, and to learn how to write a proper Yiddish sentence, but how would this benefit someone growing up in Poland? The question of *tachlis* (practical purpose) loomed large, and if Zionists claimed that their Hebrew schools prepared young Jews for life in the Palestinian, Hebrew-speaking homeland, the Tsisho schools could make no such assertions.

While modern Yiddish culture in the inter-war period found a center in Poland, modern Hebrew culture fared less well. The Hebrew press, supported by the Zionist movement, was not nearly as successful as its Yiddish rival, inasmuch as the new Hebrew theater and literature were now concentrated in Tel Aviv and Jerusalem rather than in Warsaw and Vilna. Hebrew, of course, was not a spoken language of Polish Jewry, and in an age of mass-circulation newspapers and novels, the small, cultural elite which had traditionally supported Hebrew culture could not compete with popular tastes and habits. Nonetheless, the idea of promoting a modern Hebrew culture in Poland did lead to the establishment of the remarkable *Tarbut* (Culture) school system, backed by the General Zionists and other, moderate, left-wing Zionist parties. They undertook the awesome task of making Hebrew a living language for elementary and high school pupils. Hebrew was the medium of instruction for all subjects save Polish language and history. With the establishment of Tarbut kindergartens and high schools it became possible for Polish Jews to spend their entire educational career in a Hebrew-speaking environment. In effect, these schools became islands of Hebrew speech and culture, drawing inspiration from the rapidly developing modern Hebrew educational opportunities in Palestine.

In the final analysis, from a linguistic point of view, the Tarbut schools were more alien to Polish Jewry than were the Tsisho institutions. On the other hand, inasmuch as the Zionist schools were less radical politically, and more closely related to traditional Jewish education and values, they were readily maintained by a relatively small group of enthusiasts.

* * *

Chapter IX

Chaim Zhitlovsky (1865-1943) was the standard-bearer of Diaspora nationalism and Yiddishist secularism. Shortly after World War I he pointed out that since the turn of the century Jewish Socialists sought to aid their laboring brethren not only as Jews, but primarily as human beings. However, as they became more involved, it dawned on them that Socialism is an international movement whose underlying aim is to obliterate nationalistic distinctions and fuse all mankind into a homogeneous whole, while assuming that each society should have the opportunity to display its uniqueness. Further, it proposed that all people abide together in peace, stand side by side in the battle against Nature and the vagaries of living, and make certain that one group does not dominate another. Socialism does not allow for elitism, there is no qualitative difference between societies. Each has its virtues and defects. Each has something to offer, and can learn from the other.

As Jewish Socialists sharp-focused on their brethren, they realized that they were neither better nor worse than other peoples; that they have a claim to a distinctive life-style, and are a vital part of the human race. However, instead of civil rights, as also demanded by the bourgeoisie at the time, they sought to achieve one of the highest ideals of the Jewish people – *national* equality. They were also convinced that sooner or later all international Socialists will accept this concept, which was, in essence, a basic aspect of the movement's ideology, and lend the Jews a hand towards gradually reaching this goal. The aspirations of the Jewish people were, in effect, bound to the destiny of the ever increasing working class.

In this regard, Zhitlovsky hoped that the folk literature created by the younger generation of Jewish writers would continue to develop, while attracting new talents, and would ultimately rise to the level of Europe's most important literary works. He further maintained that as the literature will be enriched with books on a variety of sciences, the need for authors' recognition from outside sources would diminish considerably. Their emotions and untrammeled thoughts would blossom in their own home and be expressed in their own language. All their creations in the arts and sciences would be articulated in Yiddish. Yiddish culture and education would proliferate endlessly, and become an important factor in binding the intelligentsia with the common man, while uniting all Jews throughout the Diaspora.

He went even further by urging that the Jewish proletariat of various lands combine forces and create a general, independent, labor association which would protect Jewish interests, as well as those of the people among whom they dwelt, thereby hastening the day of Socialism and liberty. In this free Socialist society the Jew would be able to live out his distinctive life-style, with schools, competently administered *hedorim* (religious elementary schools), gymnazia and Real schools, even universities. If three million Swiss can maintain ten institutions of higher learning, he contended, why should not eight million Yiddish speaking Jews be able to support a score of universities? Thus they would become one of the best educated folk in the world, and Jews everywhere, whether it be Vilna, Warsaw or New York, would be proud of their learning and culture; would cherish the resulting refinement and motivation toward advancement; would gladly interface with the cultivated of mankind.

Eventually, he concluded, the nations would come to appreciate that the Jewish people is not inferior to them, is capable of plucking the finest fruits of European civilization, adapting it to new forms and returning the principle with interest to its source. And if it is destined that some day, in the dim, dim future, all the nations of the world would fuse into an indistinguishable whole, Jews likewise would lose their identity. But until that point in time the Jewish people will continue to hold its rightful place in the scheme of history.

At the other end of the secularist spectrum *Ahad Ha'am* (Asher Ginsburg – 1856-1927) played a major role in the Jewish national movement of the time, and as an essayist with a lucid Hebrew style advocated its primacy over Yiddish, which he denigrated as a primitive *jargon*.

He taught that the nation is the people's "ego," i.e., its internal creative force, the sum total of its memory and will for survival. The urge to live is an instinctive power, a mighty, irrational force of nature that stems from the unconscious areas of the soul. In order to survive, the Jewish people must strengthen its national will. This can be achieved in two ways that complement each other: by establishing colonies in *Eretz Yisroel* (Palestine), and by fortifying the national spirit of the people, which finds expression in its national culture and destiny.

He strongly maintained that the Jewish national, vital ardor finds eloquence primarily in morality, not religion. To him the religious beliefs and practices of Judaism are but the external garb of the intuitive and unique, moral convictions of the Jewish people. The creation of suitable conditions for the survival of the Jewish spirit was the main concern of Ahad Ha'Am's thought. In essence, Jewish vitality depends not on Judaism, but rather on its national ethics. Thus he reformulated fundamental Jewish concepts and gave them a modern slant: "national will" instead of Providence; ethics in place of divine inspiration. In this context he mercilessly dissected the servile stance of the assimilated intelligentsia whose vitiated Jewish values resulted from a feeble mimicry of the host cultures in which they lived.

When Ahad Ha'am wrote about the "national will" he did not mean "Zionism" in the generally accepted sense of the term. He held that a solution to the Jewish problem can be found primarily in the creation of an ideal, an aspiration, which would offset the Jewish people's protracted misery. Judaism could recover its inner freedom only in the land of Israel, the land where the Jewish people was born and where the Jewish right to reside was beyond question. He is, therefore, identified with the doctrine of Zion as a "spiritual center" for modern Jewry, which would be, by his definition, a well-rounded and creative Jewish society in Palestine, freed from the pressures of conformity to a dominant Gentile majority, and would exert a spiritual effect on Jewry everywhere, radiating "to the great circumference, to all the communities of the Diaspora, to inspire them with new life and preserve the overall unity of the Jewish people."

He consistently maintained that the national rather than the religious character of Judaism was fundamental. He labeled the philosophical position of emancipated western Jews that Judaism was a system of eternal religious verities as "spiritual slavery under the veil of outward freedom." He was especially critical of the tenet that the Jewish right to survive was dependent primarily on a mission to teach ethical monotheism in the Diaspora. Western Jews had been willing to efface their identity as a living people for the sake of political rights as individuals. The resulting loss of self-pride, he insisted, was to be contrasted with the attitude of East European Jewry of his time, which he described as "inner freedom despite outer slavery." In effect, strong Jewish ethnic loyalty in face of Czarist restrictive laws. Moreover, the western notion implied that Jewishness was a rational decision made after a thorough investigation of religious and philosophical alternatives. This was, he felt, self-deception.

Jewish feeling was a natural sentiment that needed no such justifcation. Concern for the fate of one's people everywhere, and respect for its historical memories, was an emotion that all human beings experience, a tie ever more primary than one's rational, abstract duty to humanity at large.

Jewish identity, therefore, committed one to no particular metaphysical system, nor did it conflict with a scientific view of the cosmos. In place of theology and philosophical idealism, he turned to the social sciences, particularly Darwinian anthropology and social psychology, to explain Judaism's history. Like all organic entities, nations were collectives with a powerful, primordial "will to live," which responded to the challenges of the environment. Evolving national cultures were shaped by "innumerable causes, some permanent and some transient, not in accordance with a pattern laid down and defined at the onset." The Jewish religion was a result of the nation's instinct to adapt to its unique circumstances, and survive the vicissitudes of history. Thus, for example, Prophetic monotheism was accepted by the people during the Babylonian exile (586 BCE), according to Ahad Ha'am, because it enabled them to reject the interpretation that Israel's captivity was a victory for the conqueror's gods. Furthermore, monotheism had the advantage of guaranteeing for the exiles in Babylonia that God would save His people not only in its own land but also on foreign soil. During the medieval period, he argued, Judaism's ritual laws prevented assimilation of the people and maintained its hope in an eventual return to the Holy Land. *Hibbas Zion* (Love of Zion – a 19th century Zionist movement) and Zionism were a further instance of the principle that "the instinct of self-preservation slumbers not nor sleeps in the nation's heart" (compare Psalms 121:4). Nevertheless, although intended as a scientific explanation for Jewish existence, his "national will to live" formulation takes on some features of the religious conviction that Israel is an eternal people.

In Ahad Ha'am's plan, nations also have personalities, i.e. cultural configurations that distinguish one people from another and preserve inner continuity. By means of this conceit he returned to Jewish identity those values he was unable to affirm on solely religious grounds. In Judaism, historical evolution produced a culture that esteemed the spiritual over military force. Of all ideals, Judaism emphasized most the Prophetic idea of absolute justice. He depicted the Prophet as a "man of truth," a moral extremist who places righteousness ("truth in action") at the center of human life. The supreme Jewish Prophet is the portrait of Moses in the Bible, whose importance in the national culture can never be affected by any archeological discovery, because Moses "was created in the spirit of the Jewish people, and the Creator creates in His own image."

It was this ethical imperative that rabbinic Judaism sought to put into practice through law. The evolving moral sense of the people led to the constant reinterpretation of certain Biblical passages whose literal meaning often offended later generations. In an essay dealing with the distinction between Judaism and Christianity, Ahad Ha'am goes even further toward a rational defense of certain Jewish values by arguing that the Jewish concept of justice is more objective and universal than the Christian emphasis on mercy. Whereas mercy gives the other person precedence over self (an inverted egoism), justice demands that each individual be treated as fully equal. Even though his perception of the historical evolution of national cultures might imply a moral relativism, he was convinced that the "moral law" is an objective standard of values. Hence he did not hesitate to denounce any acts performed in the name of Zionism that conflicted with "the great moral principles for which our people lived, for which it suffered, and for which only [Jewry] thought it worthwhile to labor in order to become again a people in the land of its fathers."

Ahad Ha'am consistently defended Jewishness as a natural fact explainable only through the "genetic method" of the social sciences. Yet, in the evening of his life he concluded, by reaffirming some of the key ideas of western Jewry whose ideology he had previously so sharply criticized, that the spirit of Judaism rests in the primacy of Prophetic ethics, the moral obligation of Israel to represent justice and righteousness, and the task of creating a society that would be an example to all mankind. The crucial difference between Ahad Ha'am and earlier 19th century thinkers was that he, like *Moses Hess* (1812-1875), turned away from what seemed to them empty abstractions, toward a concrete Jewish community, renewed in its ancient land, free to order its own life and realize its original moral vision.

Still another definition of secularism was proffered by the educator/writer *Leibush Lehrer* (1887-1965), who maintained that Judaism is not only a religion, but rather an entire folk culture. Thus he challenged Chaim Zhitlovsky's definition of Yiddishism as the only unbroken, spiritual thread in Jewish life. True, there had emerged a Yiddish literature and schools as the language itself began to take on a patina of grace. However, in the final analysis, the movement failed in its appeal to the Jewish masses, having become the theoretical property of a handful of ideologues and their devoted followers. Several labor organizations advocated the extended use of Yiddish among their members, but remained indifferent, if not antagonistic, to such an ideological formulation.

Hebraism, as a pure language-ethos, suffered a similar fate, albeit a bit more accepted. As such, it evoked a great deal of enthusiasm and generated energetic activity. However, the idea of making the language pivotal to Jewish culture left most people cold. Thus Lehrer was convinced that *Language Nationalism* was much less important for Jews than it was for other peoples.

After the turn of the millenium, when Jews began to develop a sense of folk consciousness, the role of a national language was not, nor could it have been, similar to that of modern times. In the Middle Ages, the populace among whom Jews dwelt was indifferent to dialects spoken, and was unaware of the significance attached to language as a means of identifying nationality. The Jewish condition was unique in that there was the constant need for adaptation to the struggle for survival during the various waves of persecution and wandering. Under these circumstances, Lehrer pointed out, that even if Jews had had their own language, it would have clashed with the tongue of the host country and would ultimately have disappeared, thereby severing the connection with their brethren in the Diaspora.

He further noted that unlike Judaism, for most peoples religion comprised an external, supra-national component of their culture. Therefore, Yiddish might also have been considered as a peripheral phenomenon, particularly in view of its similarity to German. But it could never have displaced Hebrew as the central factor in the Jew's spiritual life, because Hebrew was the symbol of ultimate national liberation; of messianic expectation; of Zionist-Territorialist redemption. In any event, Yiddish lacked that all-important provision which made it possible for other oppressed and emerging peoples to adopt their folk tongue as the emblem of national emancipation and renaissance – their own land. Thus the soil became the seed-bed for their linguistic and cultural development, as well as the site of their struggle for independence from oppressive rulers.

As far as the Jewish people was concerned, Lehrer pointed out, such a concept of autonomy was definitely ruled out. Diaspora-nationalism hardly gripped the people, whether by a form of territorialism, or even a Messianic fantasy. Some Jews viewed nationalism as a threat to their security and distanced themselves from the group. It is precisely the tenuousness and unavoidable differences of opinion regarding Jewish nationalistic aims that created a psychological problem with regard to the language of their host country.

Late in the 1930s Lehrer wrote that most of the controversies between Yiddishists and Hebraists were as asymmetrical as the disputations between rabbis and churchmen in the Middle Ages. The Hebraists were, almost without exception, Zionists. As such, they employed Hebrew to defend only one aspect of the generally accepted solution to the Jewish problem. The Yiddishists could not claim such unanimity of feeling, so they logically and psychologically separated the language issue from the totality of Jewish cultural life, and were left with a barren idea which began and ended with itself. On the other hand, the Hebraists started with a group of conceptions which, they were convinced, would inevitably lead to the centrality of Hebrew in the thrust toward Jewish nationalistic evolution. Consequently, they presented a completely different set of fundamentals than the Yiddishists who, by this time, were far removed from the people.

Lehrer contended that secularism rejected everything that religious Jews represented. Nevertheless, he supported the view that the trend towards modernization would maintain just the opposite. True, every custom, form, ancient tradition is precious, simply because it is old, conventional, historically rooted, an integral facet of the Jewish mindset. However, the situation became problematic in face of a clash between the traditional past and the harsh reality of the contemporary life pattern.

Actually, this approach advocated support for Jewish content and values while accommodating to the rhythm of modern living. Under the circumstances, Yiddish became a part of these cultural treasures, because a language, insofar as it is a manifestation of a group's uniqueness, has a considerable impact upon the enrichment and strengthening of a people.

Sensitive to the upheavals of the 1930s, he cautioned that no one should, nor even dare to, deny that the Jewish people was passing through a perilous crisis and that the stumbling blocks in its path were not easily hurdled. But that which was right about Yiddish applied also to the Jew. The same spirit that aroused the conviction in Jewish hearts that these lowering dangers can be overcome should fire belief in the continued existence of Yiddish. The number of Yiddish speakers might decrease considerably, but its demise would strongly affirm that the Jew had not succeeded in prevailing over the threatening perils surrounding him. It would further emphasize that full-bodied Jewish life, of which a national language is merely an aspect, has ceased to function. In truth, Yiddish was born and sustained itself because Jews lived Jewishly. It was an integral part of the people's life-style, an instrument of popular cultural expression. Tragically, the Holocaust that obliterated the vital, Yiddish-speaking part of the Jewish people, convinced Lehrer that he would live out his years in a deep spiritual void.

The rather extensive literature of the inter-War years that dealt with issues related to secularism/traditionalism, almost uniformly pointed to the assumption that Jewish secularism in the Diaspora, despite those modern Jews who could not affirm theistic religion, and Judaism is God-centered, aimed at stressing that Jewishness is so complex, profound, unique and comprehensive, that every Jewish individual may discover in that symphony melodies that captivate him, and motifs which sound deep echoes in his personality. If, on occasion, secular Jews longed for values which gave meaning and sustenance to the existence of their forebears, and were sensitive to the beauty and insights of the religious creativity of their people, they did not thereby deny their secularist professions, but rather verified that both terms in the expression *secular Jews* are of equal importance. Thus they confirmed that Jewish secularism bears the imprint of the collective Jewish experience, and that, in the words of Y.L. Peretz, it looks upon the world through Jewish eyes.

Lehrer agreed with those Jewish humanists, or secularists, who realized that their most precious ideals and standards, if they are to answer the need for solace and sustenance in times of crisis, must spring from their people's unique experience and be rooted in the spiritual soil of ancestry. For secularism, like Judaism, while giving the Jew a sense of belonging, invariably draws its inspiration from the folk's sages, martyrs, traditions, hopes and aspirations. A secularism that is meaningful to the modern Jewish individual should be the result of organic development, and the fruit of a particular cultural climate. Only secularism, with tight bonds to the culture and history of his ethnic group, can give the modern Jew the mooring he seeks. Otherwise there would be fashioned another *ism*, competing with others for recognition, instead of helping in the survival and enrichment of its adherents for whom it was devised.

Most writers who dealt with the subject during this period concurred that to the secular Jew, the chief characteristic of religion in general, and of Judaism in particular, is a personal faith in a divine power that rules the universe. Obviously, a secularist could not accept such a concept despite the accident of birth to Jewish parents. However, this did not imply that he was a complete stranger to the loftiness, poetry, and universal insights which his ancestors wove into historic Judaism. If ever he experienced moments of exaltation, and yearned to transcend the limitations on the spirit of its material nature, then, in the words of *Henri Bergson* (1859-1941), the God of the Prophets, Kabbalists and Hasidim might come closer to him. But Judaism cannot be normative for the secularist as it is for a pious Jew. Jewish secularism suggested a cognizance that responded to all that was good and valuable in non-Jewish cultures, but as seen through the prism of Jewish history, which shaped both the Jewish collectivity and the individual. It appreciated that the modern Jewish secularist was *linked* to his heritage, but not *shackled* by it. As long as traditional observances and customs were not obligatory for him, but were of a voluntary nature (for the sake of anchorage for his children, or because of sentimental reverence for ancestral practices) then they were not inconsistent with his secularist philosophy.

The common denominator that characterized various statements of the 1920s and 30s, indicated that the evolution of Jewish secularism, while adapting itself to time and place, paralleled, in some respects, the development of Judaism. Just as, throughout the centuries, Jewish religion has absorbed alien influences and changed forms, institutions and ideas, so has Jewish secularism been modified by western concepts. Living in a pragmatic, pluralistic society, the establishment cannot impose a preconceived faith upon its members, but must grant them the right to choose freely those aspects of their legacy they consider pertinent to their struggles and aspirations.

Consequently, Lehrer concluded, just as a religious person must find God for himself, so the individual must seek his own way toward identification with the group. Each generation is justified in reexamining hallowed values in light of its own experience. Thus, all Jewish philosophies aimed at preservation of the group and enhancement of the individual, fall within the framework of authentic Judaism.

* * *

March 26, 1946, Niger delivered an address before the alumni and students of the Jewish Theological Seminary, New York City, entitled *What I Believe As A Jew*, in which he set forth his credo, with special emphasis on the secular/traditional aspects of Judaism.

He suggested that the terms "I...believe...Jew..." have in contemporary times a closer affinity to *Aggadah* (legend) than to *Halachah* (religious law), because the former is really a tale, a parable, a homily, or even a piece of ethical teaching, which is never as dispassionate nor as definitvely proscribed as the latter. If one has the opportunity to talk about his own beliefs, and in a confessional mode at that, then, obviously, he has no intention of being legalistically impartial. True, belief as such is not subjective, because when one believes he is no longer alone, nor need he be cautious. Withal that, faith is a personal, albeit not a strictly objective matter, inasmuch as each one believes as he sees fit, according to his own perceptions, and particularly when articulating these sentiments as a Jew.

A Jew, this has been, for some time now, an internal concept, hidden from sight, almost legendary. Niger referred, of course, to the Jew who shared his outlook, and pointed out that he lacks that full-blooded substantiality of the *Halachah-Jew*, who performs all six hundred and thirteen religious obligations, and recites at least one hundred blessings daily. He recalled from his childhood that he did not *believe* in Judaism because he *lived* it, in fact, he *was* it. His Jewish commitment was virtually the air he breathed, the piece of bread he ate, the water he drank, along with the appropriate blessing in each instance. His belief encompassed not only his own life, but also that of those near him. It was not limited to the bread he consumed, after having ritually washed his hands and recited the applicable blessing, but most important, it included the earth whence it was brought forth, as well as the heavens reverberating with lightning and thunder, for which he recited special blessings. He remembered those days vividly, when his soul, along with those of all other Jews, stood at the foot of Mount Sinai. At that moment his Jewishness was a part of this world, a piece of objective reality. Actually, Judaism was the Jews' *whole* world as well as their *total* reality. "And now as I stand before you and attempt to outline what I believe as a Jew, I realize that my Jewishness, my belief as well as myself, are actually a form of *aggadah*, with overtones of inferences, homilies, and hidden meanings, without the advantage of literal explanation."

For Niger it was obvious that the issue of one's Jewishness was not a matter of "right or wrong," of "true or false." He sensed that his generation was indeed perplexed, and would have been better off had it had the humility to *ask* the right questions. As for himself, Niger acknowledged that in the course of concentrating on the study and criticism of literature and art forms he came to understand *Henrik Ibsen*'s (1828-1906) caveat to poets and artists that their function is to ask rather than to answer. Nevertheless, he felt that from a stylistic point of view, if for no other reason, he could best present his credo in a declaratory cast.

In using the traditional Hebrew form *ani ma'amin* (I believe), Niger stated categorically that, first of all, he believes in believing. One must stand in awe of the wonders of creation, the miracles of nature, the limitless talents of man, whose soul sometimes sinks into the abyss, and on other occasions rises to the starry heavens. Yet there is a distinct difference when one looks at the world through Jewish eyes. One might travail and consider himself a Jew even without the capacity and will to believe in a supranatural being. However, it is difficult, if not impossible, for one to be a Jew while lacking the ability to believe in holiness and to conceptualize Jewish history without its martyrs.

He contended that genuine, essential Judaism, not necessarily in the religious sense, could not have survived without the foundation of belief. Consequently, it is impossible to be even an agnostic Jew unless one were sensitive to the spiritual values that lie imbedded in Jewish history, the light that shines forth from the people's destiny, existence, and struggle for survival. But how can one believe in Jewish ideals while lacking the feeling for higher, spiritual matters, or suffer for Judaism when the imagery is too poor to encompass ideas which simply cannot be comprehended by common wisdom or the five senses? One must be as comfortable with the vagaries of the real world as he is with the protective covering of the star-studded skies above, if he is to appreciate the light of Torah, the hidden warmth of Judaism. One is simply incapable of being a Jew unless he is blessed with the desire and motivation to believe, not in the theological but rather in the *teleological* meaning of the idea.

Niger was convinced that there exists a system of law and order, an awareness of human responsibility on the part of the individual to himself as well as to society. In this context he felt that as a man and a Jew, he considered the two to be one and the same, it would be most improper to formulate a Jewish credo without the primary, fundamental *ani ma'amin*: I believe in believing.

He believed, because he wanted and had to, in the existence and unalterable worth of his people. This included, likewise, the historical/nationalistic dimension, not because of any biological law of collective support, but in view of the Jew's history which had, and hopefully will continue to have, purpose and value. For the Jew, existence for its own sake is neither desirable nor necessary. An individual might persist in a bitter and devastating life only because he is afraid of dying. However, a collective, a folk, and particularly such as the Jewish people, that does not provide its sons and daughters with individual security; does not make the life of its members easier, but rather more difficult and often places them in jeopardy, must, in the eyes of the people, *merit* suffering and sacrifice. Thus, worthiness lies not only in the Jewish historical experience distinguished by features no other folk possesses, but also in contemporary life which is an innovational continuum of the lofty, uniquely Jewish past. Only the mindfulness of variegated life-experiences, moral strengths and spiritual treasures that Jews have accumulated, and continue to so do for themselves and the world (something which the more secure and stable societies could not manage), only belief in the Jewish creative, spiritual distinctiveness, could have made possible the ecstasy of those few, select individuals, and the burden of extreme devotion for the masses, that characterized the drama, the tragic glory of Jewish history.

From this viewpoint, Niger intimated, the Jews, as a people, will have to be either spiritually creative and culturally different, or world-wide they will cease to exist. Two years prior to the establishment of the State of Israel (1948), he presciently observed that even if there were to be a large settlement in the projected sovereign Jewish state, with its own political/economic structures, and its anticipated small dimensions, the people could not have a justifiable existence of any value if they were to become *k'chol hagoyim* (Hebrew: like all other peoples); if they were to break off the singular evolution of their entire historic experience, beginning with the patriarch Abraham and down to his most recent descendants.

As he pursued this thought, Niger cautioned that not only as an insignificant minority in the world at large, but in a country under its own flag, might such a people become assimilated morally. Thus the Prophets of old constantly warned the children of Israel about the dangers of spiritual and moral deterioration, of building on the Judaean hills altars dedicated to strange gods. Even in our day, he continued, we are threatened with "slavery within freedom" (see Ahad Ha'am), not only in countries of emancipation, but in the land of auto-emancipation as well (see *Leon Pinsker* – 1821-1891). Therefore, wherever Jews abide, their national strategy must be oriented toward securing the spiritual and cultural borders maximally, if possible, but certainly minimally. Mere material, land-locked frontiers do not suffice for the Jewish people. The great advantage of having a homeland lies not, as many believe, in the chance to discard time-worn burdens and become like all other folks. On the contrary. Only in his own state can the Jew have broader and fuller opportunities to assert his right and obligation toward developing the prime aspects of his historic individuality. But what are they? In his characteristic manner, Niger delineated two approaches which might answer the questions of when, where and how did the Jewish historic personality take form.

The first, which he favored, was historical/dialectical/ evolutionary. The other was dogmatic/revolutionary. The latter maintained that everything done during the last two thousand years of Jewish and world history toward development of the multifaceted Jewish national distinctiveness, was a sort of divine or historical curse that must be exorcized and rejected. That would lead to an upheaval in the Jewish life-style which was viewed by some as a truncated, unhealthy ghetto-philosophy and Diaspora-psychology. In effect, it meant excising from the historic folk-organism everything that had grown and accrued during the two-millennial Diaspora experience. In fact, several leading ideologues of this rationale, while glorifying the past, succeeded in ignoring some links (and at times whole sections) of the centuries-old heritage chain. Just as in the case of some non-Jewish renaissance movements, the leaders of Jewish national revivalism constantly harked back to the earlier epochs of their history while minimizing or entirely denying the creative accomplishments of later eras.

Niger preferred to align himself with those who held that it was the late post-Biblical, Talmudic, Geonic/rabbinic developmental periods, as well as the phases of Kabbalism and Hasidism, that shaped the body and soul of the Ashkenazic, East European centers annihilated in the Holocaust. He believed that the Jewish people, as it is known today, is in its entirety the product of the last two millenia of its history, rather than that of the first one thousand years. This is meaningful, not because it is the larger or later part, but rather because it assimilated and modified the earlier period, thereby becoming the seedbed for further growth. He also maintained that the Diaspora era was no less, and perhaps even more, *Jewish* history and heritage than the saga of the Hebrew tribes in the Promised Land, inasmuch as the seeds planted earlier sprouted and brought forth timely fruit. Indeed, it was in the Diaspora that the concept of "Israel, Torah, and The Holy One, blessed be He" were fused into one, for only then did the people of Israel became what *it* is, and Torah (Jewish culture) what *it* is.

He highlighted the significance of the transition from sacrifice to prayer, following the destruction of the Temple in 70 C.E. True, long before, the prophet Isaiah (1:11-17) understood that the Lord preferred honesty and justice rather than offerings brought by hands dripping blood. However, that was more the Prophet's idealization than a description of the people's sinful way of life. Soon thereafter devotional life was cleansed and became more enlightened; the house of the Lord was no longer stained with blood; the last vestiges of paganism disappeared, and the Jews became God's holy folk. Subsequently, the *kohanim* (Hebrew: priestly class) disappeared and the Jews became a "nation of priests." According to tradition, wherever Jews wandered during their long and tortuous exile, God's presence accompanied them, and so, in the course of many generations the sublime triad of "Israel, Torah and the Holy One, blessed be He" was crystallized.

In this sense the Prophets prepared the ground and foretold the spiritual maturation of the Jewish people, which, to the wonderment of both Jewish and world history, was revealed in the Land of Israel. Prophesy embodied the potential spiritual and moral possibilities that came to fruition in the Talmudic period (the first five centuries of the Common Era). He noted that the creators of this voluminous work were primarily Diaspora personalities, and that the spiritual standard-bearers of the nation, since the redaction of the Talmud (c. 500), were the *Geonim*, *Posekim* (Hebrew: decisers), *Kabbalists,* poets, and philosophers, who led the people through various phases of the exile.

Niger contended that these figures, in their hearts and minds, were fired by God's word and that of His Prophets, but in a completely different context. The Word had become humanized, a way of life, a religion of performance. Prophesy remained utopian, while Talmud and the *Shulchan Aruch* (Hebrew: Prepared Table, the generally accepted code of Jewish law), became, in the modern sense, practical *idealism*. Isaiah spoke about "the end of days," the messianic era, whereas all those saintly and dedicated personalities who dotted the landscape of Jewish thought and culture during the last two thousand years, did not represent visions of salvation, but rather strengths and facts of the here and now. If in Prophetic times there were revealed the hidden foundations of Judaism, it was in later generations that the magnificent structure was erected and the dream of the Prophets translated into verity.

It should be borne in mind, Niger emphasized, that truth is neither as attractive nor inspiring as augury. Yet, throughout the many waves of darkness in the two-millennial course of Jewish wandering, there somehow shone a Prophetic ray of light pointing to the "end of days," messianic times, and the fulfillment of the vision "for the earth shall be filled with knowledge of the glory of the Lord, as the waters cover the sea" (Habakkuk 2:14). Thus Jews developed into a folk of learning; an unending love of erudition; a profound respect for scholarship. In effect, their this-world was actually their world-to-come.

He likewise surmised that the Jewish people was unique in its antipathy to the sight of blood, perhaps because of, or despite the many blood libels and pogroms inflicted upon it relentlessly. Hence their own agonies made them empathetic to the suffering of others. But most important was the singular talent for perpetuating and vitalizing their distinctive language and literature (Hebrew) throughout the vagaries of the extensive Exile. Add to that the remarkable phenomenon of two sister tongues and literatures, Aramaic and Yiddish, which rounded out the Jewish propensity for creativity.

Niger suggested that while probing the past for those wellsprings which did, and indeed must, refresh the Jew's creative life, one should avoid harking back to their origin, whether it be the Land of Israel or the Diaspora, and should rather determine whether they are dried up or still gushing. It is mandatory to assess the values in every epoch, trend, and movement of Jewish history; the religious, ethical, intellectual or artistic achievements that link the Jew with his historic tradition, while not being bound by it.

He viewed as a given the need for the various streams of bygone creativity to nourish and fructify Jewish innovativeness in the present, and for all time. He was also convinced that the troublesome contradictions and inconsistencies at the root of many conflicts between differing sects and schools of thought were merely a passing phase of extremism and abrasiveness, characteristic of emerging sectarianism as it sensed indifference on the one hand, and unmitigated opposition on the other. This led, inevitably, to militancy, fanaticism and, often, outrageous conduct. However, as time went on, the sharp edges of youthful, ideological obstinacy were gradually blunted, confrontations between old and new approaches more or less settled, and former enemies became new-found friends. A valid example of the above thesis may be found in the social and cultural history of 19th century European Jewry. The first half was marked by strife between orthodox and Reform Jews in the west, as well as Hasidism and Haskalah in the east. The second half was distinguished by the clash of Socialist and nationalist ideologies.

He intimated that Hasidism had aroused intense religious feelings which were on the verge of becoming congealed, while revealing new sources of faith that excited the masses and stimulated the creative imagination of individuals. The Haskalah, on the other hand, liberated the Jew's thought process and showed him the way to modern culture. Obviously, the unfettered thinking of one portion of the population, alongside the kindled religious fervor of another large group, could hardly have made for compatibility. It appeared to be a war to the bitter end, with no quarter given from either side.

However, Niger pointed out, the second half of the century portended a different scenario. There was evolving nationalist consciousness on one side, and the Socialist idea making inroads to the Jewish community on the other, two new ideologies struggling with each other and striving for domination. While it seemed they were irreconcilable, by the turn of the century it became apparent that there was no contradiction between the battle for social justice and the Jewish national renaissance. On the contrary, there was a confluence of social and national aspirations. Hence, not only did this bitter partisanship come to an end, but the energies of former ideology-enemies, Hasidism and Enlightenment, were channeled into them, while each movement retained its identity. In effect, Jewish nationalism merged the deep longing for redemption of Hasidism with the modernistic, cultural ideas of rationalism. Thus the image of a Jewish Socialist, Folkist or pioneer was the product of the crucible which fused social awareness with nationalistic self-consciousness. He cautioned, however, that in light of the onerous trials and tribulations the Jewish people had endured during this period it would have been the height of folly to shatter that delicate synthesis achieved through such tireless effort and devotion.

Niger considered it ironic that after the cataclysmic upheavals in Jewish life during the first half of this century, there might still be those who view the Enlightenment with scorn, despite its important place in Jewish social history, and urged a return to orthodoxy, even the ghetto. Perhaps they yearned for those "good old" pre-emancipation times when they were comfortable in their isolation and rigid life-style. But he was adamant in the belief that despite the arduous travail the understanding reached between yesterday and today, tradition and reform, Jewish national consciousness and civil rights, the Jew and his fellow human beings, the nation and mankind – all these can and must remain intact.

With almost prophetic vision he stated categorically that the Jewish national renaissance would have been impossible, both in the Diaspora and Israel, had not the tremendous gains of rationalism and enlightenment been preserved. However, he admitted that in contemporaneous times (1946), and in light of recent events, the wondrous fruits of the Tree of Knowledge (Gen. 2:9) undoubtedly appeared rotten, poisonous, and accursed. Withal that, he was unshaken in the belief that the day will come when once again human creativity will grow and blossom. At the same time he cautioned that both as individuals and as a people, Jews would be the first victims of neo-barbarism, anywhere in the world, if the banners of liberty and equality were to be destroyed. Denying the ideals of personal freedom and social justice, or even minimizing them, would constitute a death sentence, not only in the Diaspora, but in the Land of Israel as well.

The war against totalitarianism and all it represented must continue, Niger persisted, even after defeating the inhuman dictators. Otherwise, all that the Jew had achieved, including the Yishuv in Palestine, would be in lowering danger. It should be borne in mind that the Jewish State, when it comes into being, will not be able to serve as an ark of rescue from the flood (Gen. 6:14). Actually, the Jewish people could not have shared in what it possesses, nor could it have turned out to be what it is, were it not for those monumental, historic movements which burst the walls and shattered the foundations of their social and cultural isolation. Without the Haskalah the Jew would have been deprived of Yiddish Socialism, settlement in Palestine, or even the idea of a Jewish State. Political Zionism stemmed not only from traditional messianic longing, but primarily from European revolutionary, nationalist, socialist aspirations. *Moses Hess* (1812-1875), *Perez Smolenskin* (1842-1885), *Moses Leib Lilienblum* (1843-1910), *Leo Pinsker* (1821-1891), *Ahad Ha'am* (1856-1927), *Theodor Herzl* (1860-1904), all were products of enlightenment and emancipation. Their attitude towards rationalism and human rights was more critical than dogmatic, because they were Jews of their times who had a closer tie to modern Zionism than, for example, *Rabbi Isaac Luria* (1534-1572) or *Reb Menahem Mendel of Vitebsk* (1730- 1788), proponents of mystical, messianic yearning.

Jewish autoemancipation, Niger claimed, was simply an extension of the European emancipation atmosphere and, like its source, could succeed only by virtue of self-perpetuation. Even present-day orthodoxy, to say nothing about neo-orthodoxy, could not do without the *means* resulting from the advancement and modernization of Jewish life, despite the fact that they referred to the *ends* with derision and ingratitude. It might almost be superfluous to list, he noted, the various manifestations of modern religious and nationalist Judaism for which they were indebted to the non-Jewish world; for the ideas and movements which brought them into contact with science, literature, art, and society at large. Without these dynamic influences Jews would never have developed *chochmes Yisroel* (Hebrew: the scientific and critical study of Jewish literary sources), their bi-lingual literatures, theater, sculpture, painting, the plastic arts, as well as many other facets of human expression which enhance the life rhythm of a people.

Niger firmly believed it would be erroneous to deduce from the Holocaust that modern culture betrayed the Jewish people and, therefore, must be rejected. On the contrary. The lessons learned from those horrendous events indicated that the culture which promised, and in many instances delivered justice and freedom, simply failed to shore up its social and moral potentiale globally, and for all time. He emphasized that there was no cause for alarm, its goal had simply not yet been demonstrably achieved, in view of the zigzag course and temporary downhill slide. Admittedly, in attempting to accelerate mankind's intellectual growth, modern culture created a crisis in its ethical and religious consciousness. Thanks to science, art, and technology, man's collective experience had been expanded without refining the emotional fabric of the individual, thus causing the external progress of the group to overtake the slower pace of personal humanism. He sensed that there was a disturbing asymmetry in general culture which made for Nazism and its incredible bestiality, as well as the total disintegration of the period. This justified the motivation to do battle against the unwholesomeness and inner immaturity of global civilization, but not the world itself, for it has been the Jew's strongest support, his brightest hope. No one needs it more than a small, powerless people.

According to Niger, anti-Semitism was not the product of a defective culture or an unique cause, but rather of a number of sources drawn from a series of poisoned wells. Hence it would be impossible to cure the disease of Judaphobia by means of a single remedy. Therefore, he suggested, the Jew's strategy, with regard to his enemies should not be confined to futile attempts aimed at changing their minds. Instead, every effort should be made to heighten the impact of that minority among the nations which long ago left the jungle, so that they might help their fellow man to desist from crawling morally on all fours. Another antidote would be the Jew's power of resistance, the capacity to retrieve the talent of previous generations to sublimate their suffering, the travail of a lamb among wolves and convert physical weakness into spiritual strength.

In the final analysis, Niger observed, the Jew must combine forces with his non-Jewish friends, not with the intention of rejecting anti-Semitic allegations and challenging false accusations, but for the avowed purpose of altering those conditions in the world at large, and particularly in Jewish life, that render it possible for the foe to pass from words to deeds.

He was troubled by the question whether or not the Jew was too involved in the dichotomy of "we" and "they," and not enough with himself. It appeared that the preponderance of Jewish social and intellectual activities were externally oriented while neglecting the internal person. He stressed the fact that Jews must focus their attention on the innermost aspects of their life-style. True, there is need for self-protection. But woe unto such a society that is so enmeshed in self-insulation that it has neither time nor energy for self-development, self-criticism and self-advancement. He insisted that he referred not merely to some aspects of Jewish life, but to its entirety, both in the Diaspora and the Land of Israel. Actually, he hinted at an integrated Judaism in time as well as place, whereby the various epochs of Jewish history would be an open book and the treasures hidden therein would become a dynamic force in the Jew's cultural devlopment. This applied most urgently to the contemporary Jewish scene.

With regard to the historic past, he commented, there are those who might possibly choose the period of the first Jewish Commonwealth and its hegemony over the Land of Israel as a point of departure. Others might prefer the Diaspora era of the last two millenia. However, it is unimaginable to claim that either of these two epochs by itself represents the essence of Jewish history. The same applies to preferential exclusivity regarding a specific geographical settlement. Consequently, it would be as simplistic to compress the totality of Jewish living and aspirations into the framework of the national homeland as it would to limit the distinctive Jewish life-style only to the Diaspora.

The difference between Zionists and non-Zionists, Niger maintained, dare not be predicated on the total denigration of the Diaspora by the former, nor on the minimizing of the hopes and achievements in the Land of Israel by the latter. The distinction might be a matter of emphasis or nuance, but no more. He allowed for a Zionist to hold, in the spirit of Ahad Ha'am, that "out of Zion shall go forth the Law" (Isaiah 2:3), and that the revitalized society in the Land of Israel, together with its cultural advances, would bolster the Jewish sense of security in the Diaspora. But he also envisioned a Jewish philosophy and program where the core would not be the homeland, but rather the Jews as a global people. This would not eliminate the Land of Israel from the world map, for it would be a beacon unto the Diaspora. However, Niger conceded, while he could not foretell the future, it must be recognized that the achievements, as well as hidden potential of the Yishuv so far, are products of the material and spiritual forces gathered in the Diaspora. All the pioneers, builders, leaders, and creative talents came from from here to there, and not the reverse. The many spiritual and psychological values found in the Yishuv, including attachment to the land, unbridled optimism and the penchant for self-sacrifice, were brought by Jews from the four corners of the globe. Even the antipathy toward and denial of the exile were borrowed, thereby forming a grotesque, tragic paradox in the Jewish psyche.

Niger's Zionist sentiments were anchored in the profound certainty that the deeper the Jew became rooted in the soil of Israel, and the longer the two-millenia old seeds of folk and world experience germinated and grew, the sooner would the people enjoy the fruits of renaissance in their own homeland. He considered the State of Israel and the Diaspora to be a thesis and antithesis of tentative duration, the result of the pioneering phase of development, which, by its nature, is militant and extremist. However, he was fully convinced that sooner or later there will evolve a synthesis of Israeli and Diaspora culture, as well as an accommodation and harmonization between traditionalism and secularism. This likewise referred to the two languages characteristic of Jewish culture, Hebrew in Israel and Yiddish in the Diaspora.

To the end of his days, Niger, the Jew, the optimist, maintained that despite the many heart-rending experiences which might easily have turned a believing Jew into an agnostic, or even an atheist; regardless of the depraved human condition, there will come a turn-about, and mankind will once again embark on its inevitable uphill climb. In any event, for the Jew, he sighed, it is not the end of the world, but rather the termination of one epoch and the beginning of another, with its illusions and potentialities.

Epilogue

In an astounding quirk of history it took little more than a decade from the *Czernowitz Conference* (1908), where Jews debated among themselves whether or not Yiddish is to be considered the national language, to the *Versailles Peace Conference* (1919), where, for the first time in history, the leading powers of the world integrated the religious, national, and language minority rights of Jews into the treaty that concluded World War I.

The treaty was an attempt to establish a "just" peace, to organize Europe on national lines, and to guarantee the rights of those minorities which remained. There was ample precedent for incorporating clauses into peace agreements protecting religious minorities. It should be noted that it was the *Committee of Jewish Delegations*, in search of religious and also more general assurances, that provided the driving force behind the movement for minority treaties. Because of the large Jewish population in Poland, the Committee was anxious to extract some pledges from that state in particular. The Powers deemed this the proper place to start, in view of the many Polish problems involved in making peace with Germany. In the *Treaty of Versailles*, Poland obligated herself to embody in a pact with the Allied Powers "such provisions as may be deemed necessary...to protect the interests of inhabitants of Poland who differ from the majority of the population in race, language or religion." This *Minority Treaty*, as well as the Treaty of Versailles, was signed on June 28, 1919.

Two new premises for collective Jewish living were set forth in the agreement. First was the Palestine Mandate granted to Great Britain which, within a generation, developed into the State of Israel, and second, the concept of minority rights for diverse groups within the various states.

This prestigious forum arrived at an advanced definition of sovereignty that negated the traditional notion of empire, dependent upon a homogeneous population. In its stead came a number of national entities with cultural, ethnic, and religious minorities.

In the deliberations of all previous peace assemblies the Jewish issue was, at best, peripheral. Not at the *Congress of Vienna*, 1815 (after the Napoleonic wars), nor at the *Aix-la-Chapelle* Conference, 1818 (the formation of the Congress System), nor even at the *Congress of Berlin*, 1878 (end of the Russo-Turkish war), did Jews participate as delegates to the official sessions. The corridors of all these gatherings were crowded with lobbyists and dealers (including some non-Jews) who sought to wheedle a mite of protection for their people. In the main, these were exercises in futility.

The Versailles Conference, on the other hand, ushered in a new chapter in Jewish history. This time Jews were not merely interceders, but came as folk-representatives, duly elected by national assemblies, conferences and congresses. They had a mandate and a program. The East European deputation arrived, not with vague supplications, but with firm, carefully detailed Jewish nationalist demands, which had been crystallized over a span of four decades. Likewise, the American delegation brought a clearly itemized list of conclusions reached during discussions at the American Jewish Congress, held in Philadelphia, December 15-18, 1918. As was anticipated, the respective outlooks on Jewish life clashed internally, resulting in heated discussions and strained relationships among the leaders, but in no way minimized the unanimity of purpose.

The nationalist Jewish platform presented at the Peace Conference included the following planks: cultural and personal autonomy; a government ministry for Jewish affairs; a national board to represent the Jews; a committee of world-wide Jewry to have standing within the League of Nations. One of the cardinal requirements was for self-determination in the area of education and the right to employ Yiddish, not only in schools, but also in the courts and all other administrative agencies. The various memoranda and proposals presented to the commissions of the Conference contained the demand for full rights for Yiddish, despite the fact that the Jewish delegations included ardent Hebraists, Zionists, non-Zionists, and Socialists.

It should be noted that parallel to the consideration of the role of Yiddish, agreement had been reached on the "Sabbath-rest for Jews" issue, despite the conflicting positions of the American delegation which opposed the idea, and the British group which favored it. Ironically, it was the support of American *President Woodrow Wilson* (1856-1924) which carried the day, so that the resolution was included as Article 11 of the minority rights pact with Poland.

A memorandum listed as "Document 822," presented by Jewish delegates to the Commission on New States, contained Point #4 which ordered that each person has the right to employ his own language in public assemblies, the press and schools; that the worth of a document shall not be disqualified because of the language in which it appears; and that all previous language restrictions be annulled. An addendum referring to the establishment of state financed Jewish schools was bogged down in the discussion over who would be responsible for organizing and managing such a system. In this regard it was proposed that administration and supervision be in the hands of a national Jewish body. Subsequently, the brief was subjected to exhausting analysis by the American delegates to the Commission on New States before it was brought to the ranking body of the Conference for determination.

Meanwhile, the Commission had been inundated with protest telegrams from various government leaders, particularly Prime Minister of Poland, *Ignaz Jan Paderewski* (1860-1941), who defiantly stated that he would not sign the Peace Treaty unless the minority rights provisions were eliminated. Recognizing the difficulties of compromise, the Commission members transmitted their recommendations, along with a projected rejoinder to Paderewski, to the supreme council for its decision.

However, in the course of his unanticipated appearance at the Conference on June 27, 1919, Paderewski requested that wording of the paragraph relating to Jewish schools be altered. He agreed to finance educational institutions where religious needs would be respected and Yiddish treated as a second language. *David Lloyd George* (1863-1945), Prime Minister of Great Britain, suggested that this position went beyond the original proposal in the Treaty, while President Wilson voiced his understanding that Yiddish might be the language of instruction in elementary schools only, but should not be taught as a separate tongue. Ironically, it was *Lord Arthur James Balfour* (1848-1930), author of the famous Declaration which viewed "with favour the establishment in Palestine of a national home for the Jewish people," who objected strenuously to national rights for Polish Jewry. After a series of revisions, the sections referring to Jewish schools as included in the Minority Rights Treaty, read as follows:

Article 8: Polish citizens who belong to ethnic, religious, or linguistic minorities shall be treated both *de jure* and *de facto* like all other Polish citizens. Specifically, they shall have equal right to establish, administer, and control, at their own expense, charitable organizations, religious and social institutions, schools and other educational units, with full right to employ their own language and observe their religious customs without restriction.

Article 9: In those states and districts where there is a proportionately large number of Polish citizens who speak languages other than Polish, the Polish government must provide, within its public education system, such acceptable conditions that would enable children of Polish citizens, at the elementary level, to receive instruction in their own language. This provision shall not prevent the Polish government from making it obligatory that they also study Polish in these schools.

In those states and districts where there is a proportionately large number of Polish citizens who belong to racial, religious, or linguistic minorities, the minorities are entitled to receive an appropriate share of funds allocated by the Government, State administration, or any other budgetary source, for religious or charitable purposes, to be disbursed at their discretion.

Article 10: Local education committees to be established by the Jewish communities of Poland, will, under supervision of the Government, control distribution of the public funds proportionately designated for the Jewish schools in accord with Article 9, as well as organizing and administering them. The stipulations of Article 9 concerning the use of language in schools, apply equally to the Jewish schools.

The Poles bitterly resented having been coerced into signing the Minority Treaty. They regarded it as an intolerable act of interference on the part of the great powers and blamed the Jews for having engineered its acceptance. The Treaty was ratified by the *Sejm* (Polish parliament) only after all shades of opinion had denounced it. Its text was first published by the Polish government in its official organ more than a year later.

The secular national Jewish leadership, on the other hand, regarded its passage as a great victory. According to the optimistic Zionists it was a "Magna Carta" in that it specifically referred to Jews as a minority with national, not only religious, rights. It signified, so they thought, the beginning of a new era in Polish-Jewish relations and a foundation upon which the glorious edifice of Jewish national autonomy in Poland would be erected.

The minorities system represented a remarkable experiment in international control that lasted some twenty years. With all its faults, substantive and procedural, it could have developed into a major force for minority protection. However, it soon crumbled, along with the *League of Nations* that sponsored it. The system should have helped prevent serious disturbances by providing minorities an outlet for resolving grievances and serving as a brake on oppressive chauvinism. However, the essential weakness lay in the refusal of the states with minorities to act on their international pledges of good faith. Some of the practical provisos of the Treaty lacked precision. The procedure for hearing complaints was faulty. The League itself did not pursue recalcitrant states with proper vigor. In 1934 the world was stunned by the declaration of the Polish Minister for Foreign Affairs, *Col. Jozef Beck* (1894-1944), renouncing minority obligations. The whole structure toppled along with the League of Nations. World War II put an abrupt end to the experiment, as it did to Jewish life in Poland.

Afterword

Beyond any doubt, many of the issues dealt with in this study, and particularly that of secularism, resonate throughout Jewish life in our day. But that would have to be another undertaking.

I intended to depict a phenomenal instant in Jewish history whose bittersweet existence left an indelible impress on Jewish life. Thus, one must sadly countenance the fact that after an unique, fleeting century, the circle of Yiddish cultural endeavor is almost closed. Yes, there are some tentative efforts at continuation on a few university campuses. One still hears an impoverished language in the streets of Hasidic communities. There are half-hearted attempts at retaining the parallelism of *golus* (exile) Yiddish with *loshin koidish* (Hebrew: holy tongue) in the yeshives. But never again will there be a press which rages against the inequities and injustices of the times, while striking a note of hope and aspiration for the liberation of the Jewish people. Never again will a theater reverberate with thunderous applause in appreciation of an authentic, original drama delivered in stentorian tones. Never again will poets touch the heart with their verse, nor composers move the spirit with song, nor novelists fire the imagination with their prose. Never again will eager, young researchers juggle philologic subtleties and semantic nuances as they did in the halcyon days of the *YIVO Institute for Jewish Research*, where this writer once served as Executive Secretary. Never again will scholars meticulously investigate and eloquently chronicle the life-style, culture, and history of the Jewish people, with all its achievements and defeats. Never again will the Jew laugh at himself with tears in his eyes, while pondering the exquisite anguish of living.

In memory of a world that was precipitously and catastrophically consigned to the oblivion of history, this is a moment for *Hallel* – a prayer of praise – as well as one for *Kaddish* – a prayer for the dead.

Index of Names

Aaron Ben-Samuel 57
Abraham 70
Adam 50
Aesop 58
Sholom Aleichem 13, 27, 37, 68, 76, 92
Dante Alighieri 54
Reb Anshel of Cracow 59
Sholem Asch 26, 71, 76, 90
Pavel Axelrod 73
Baal Machshoves 69
Rabbi Israel Baal Shem Tov 57, 62, 89
Bahya 55
Majer Balaban 91
Lord Arthur James Balfour 116, 117
Bashevis (see Isaac Bashevis Singer)
Colonel Josef Beck 118
R. Dov Ber of Lyadi 57
Micha Josef Berdichewsky 68
Henri Bergson 101
H.D. Berkowitz 26
Chaim Nachman Bialik 46, 55, 68
Dr. Nathan Birnbaum 66, 67, 68, 76
Solomon Bloomgarden (Yehoash) 27
Giovanni Boccacio 54
Louis Brandeis 21
Buchboim 76

Abraham Cahan 27
Carnegie 13
Samuel Charney (see NIGER)
Rabbi Zvi Hirsh Chotch 60
Hermann Cohen 42
Dr. Abraham Coralnick 26, 31
Czernowitz Language Conference
   (1908) 6, 46, 65-72, 76, 77, 114
Jacob Dineson 66
Simon Dubnow 69
Eisic Meir Devenishki 6
William Edlin 26
Dr. Isidore Eliashev 68, 69
A.M. Evalenko 66
Ezra 50
Mordecai Fierberg 68
Josephus Flavius 50
Esther Frumkin 69, 76
Moishe Frankfurt 58
Israel Friedkin 25
Saadia Gaon 42
Solomon Ibn Gebirol 42, 55
David Lloyd George 116
Asher Ginsburg (see Ahad Ha'am)
Abraham Goldberg 67
Jacob Gordon 66
Shmarye Gorelik 6

Ahad Ha'am (Asher Ginsburg) 34, 42, 72, 94, 95, 96, 97, 105, 110, 112

Yehudah Halevi 42, 55

Dr. Alexander Harkavy 28, 32, 66

Theodor Herzl 20, 110

Moses Hess 97, 110

Dr. Benzion Hoffman (Tzivion) 67

Isaac 42, 70

Rabbi Moses Isserles 61

Jacob 70

Rabbi Jose 49

L. Khazanovich 76

Dr. Joseph Klausner 83

Leon Kobrin 27

Philip Krantz 28

Yonah Kreppel 76

Leibush Lehrer 97, 98, 99, 100, 101

M. Leontiev 28

Abraham Liessen 28

Moses Leib Lilienblum 110

Rabbi Isaac Luria 110

Baal Machshoves 68, 69

Moses Maimonides 42, 55, 84

Reb Menahem of Vitebsk 110

Julius Martov 73

Moses Mendelssohn 63

Abraham Menes 43

Morgan 13

R. Nahman of Bratzlav 57, 62

Samuel Niger (Samuel Charney) 5-8, 20, 26, 32-41, 49, 50, 54, 56, 60, 79, 82, 84-87, 102-113 (What I Believe as a Jew)

H.D. Nomberg 76

Joseph Opatashu 27

M. Osherowitz 26

Ignaz Ian Paderewski 116

Y.L. Peretz 41, 66, 70, 76, 90, 92, 100

Francesco Petrarch 54

Leon Pinsker 105

David Pinski 65, 66

Rabbi 49

Rashi 61, 83

Rav 50

Abraham Reisin 27

Rockefeller 13

Abraham Rosenfeld 26

Morris Rosenfeld 67

Samuel Rosenfeld 26

Yona Rosenfeld 26

Saul Safire 27

Jacob Saperstein 25

Ignacy Schipper 91

Zalman Schneour 26

Mendele Mocher Seforim 68, 76

Isaac Bashevis Singer 90

I.J. Singer 26, 90

Perez Smolenskin 110

Baruch Spinoza 42

Leon Trotsky 73

Y.Y. Trunk 90

William Tyndale 53

Tzivion 67

Vanderbilt 13

Oizer Varshavsky 90

A. Veiter (Eisic Meir Devenishki) 6

Morris Weinberg 26

Max Weinreich 45

Woodrow Wilson (President) 116

Yehoash (See also Solomon Bloomgarden)

R. Levi Yitzhok of Berditchev 57

R. Zelig the Kabbalist 60

Dr. Chaim Zhitlovsky 26, 41, 42, 66, 67, 68, 76, 92, 93, 94, 97

Israel Zinberg 83

Index of Publications

American Hebrew 67
Chicago Courier 25
Der Neier Geist (The New Spirit) 28
Der Tog (The Day) 7, 25, 26, 27, 31
Der Yud (The Jew) 78
Di Neie Zeit (The New Time) 28
Di Voch (The Week) 7
Di Zeit (The Times) 25
Di Zukunft (The Future) 28
Di Freie Gezelshaft (The Free Society) 28
Die Wahrheit (The Truth) 25, 31
Dos Yidische Folk (The Jewish People) 78
Emes (Truth) 81
Forward 7, 25, 26, 27, 32, 67
Freie Arbeter Shtimme (Free Workers Voice) 28
Freiheit (Freedom) 25

Haynt (Today) 90
Kultur un Bildung (Culture and Education) 7
Literrarische Monetshrift (Literary Monthly) 6
Moment (Moment) 90
Morgen Journal (Morning Journal) 25, 26, 27
Nu Yorker Yidishe Folkstzaytung (New York Yiddish Folk-newspaper) 19
Oktyaber (October) 81
Shtern (Star) 81
Socialistishe Arbeter Zeitung (Socialist Workers Newspaper) 28
Tageblat (Daily Bulletin) 25
Yidishe Journal (Jewish Journal) 25
Yidishe Shtimme (Jewish Voice) 25
Yidishe Welt (Jewish World) 25